NO THANKS, I DON'T DRINK.
MY NEW MANTRA

NO THANKS, I DON'T DRINK. MY NEW MANTRA

ASHLEE DUNN

One Time Productions, LLC

ONE TIME PRODUCTIONS, LLC
113 MEDINA STREET
MELBOURNE BEACH, FL 32951
WWW.ONETIMEPRODUCTION.COM

Cover and Interior design by Graham Hoof
Ashlee girl concept by Hampton Thrower

9 8 7 6 5 4 3 2 1

FIRST EDITION
Printed in the United States of America

LIBRARY OF CONGRESS-IN-PUBLICATION DATA

Name: Ashlee Dunn, 1970- author.
Title: No Thanks, I Don't Drink. My New Mantra / Ashlee Dunn
Description: First | Melbourne Beach, 2020
Identifiers: LCCN: 2020925738 ISBN 9781736390108 (trade paperback)
Subjects: Self Help | Health

This book is dedicated to my parents.

CONTENTS

To know what you prefer instead of humbly saying Amen to what the world tells you you ought to prefer, is to have kept your soul alive.

Robert Louis Stevenson

Letter to Reader:

Words have power. A mantra is a word or sound that you repeat in order to help with concentration/meditation. I have been a yoga teacher for 25 years and have used various mantras in my own practice. "No Thanks, I Don't Drink" isn't a typical yogic mantra, but it is one that has served me very well.

Traditionally you receive a mantra from a teacher, but this one came to me through my own meditation. Somehow saying this phrase gave me power. I didn't repeat it while meditating like you normally would with a mantra. I just started saying it to myself when I thought of it. I decided this was the phrase I would use when people offered me alcohol. What I noticed after doing this for a while is that my brain started to believe it. I found it easier and easier to just say, "No thanks." I started this process after having been a drinker for 35 years. The results were amazing.

The power of the mind is incredible. My hope is that this book will help you retrain your own mind regarding how it views alcohol. Eventually helping you to overcome the habitual pattern of drinking.

In love and light,

Ashlee

INTRODUCTION

Alcohol is a thief. A thief of all things good. Alcohol robbed me of my dignity, my spirit, my time, my personal power, my self-esteem, and virtually any other redeeming qualities I possessed. In essence, it robbed me of my true nature for most of my life. I regularly opened the door to this thief and let him in. I willingly continued to allow alcohol to rob me of all that was important to me. The truth is, I am not alone. More friends than I can count are currently in the same situation. They are stuck in an abusive relationship with alcohol. They feel this way because alcohol is an addictive, toxic poison that has the potential to ruin your life. I think for most of us who decide to break up with alcohol, there are many moments leading up to the final decision. Just like any relationship, it often takes time to hit your personal breaking point. This was definitely the case with me. I mulled the decision over for years, but I just couldn't imagine living life without wine and champagne.

I now read that statement and find it so sad. I feel lifetimes away from the person who couldn't imagine a life without alcohol. I remember how powerless, hopeless, and depressed she was. Alcohol encouraged me to be stubborn, argumentative, lazy, enslaved, deadened, aloof and in pain. Society tells us drinking makes you happy and this is just not true. During my drinking years, I thought maybe alcohol was the cause of some of my depression, but until I stopped for good, I really had no idea how much it was damaging my entire life. More than anything, my psychological addiction to alcohol was robbing me of my personal power, which affected all aspects of my life. This psychological addiction happened slowly over a long period of time. Unlike meth or heroin, or other drugs that hook you right away. Alcohol is a sneaky drug. One day you can take it or leave it and then suddenly not having it isn't something you even want to fathom. It is at this juncture where the smart decision is to completely walk away and never look back.

Just like walking away from an abusive relationship when all the signs are there before getting punched in the face. If you don't walk away from alcohol, it has the potential to destroy you and those around you. You might not see it coming, but if you can take an honest look, become mindful and start watching your patterns around your drinking, you can quit before the terrible destruction happens. Hopefully you have found this book because you are starting to take an honest (even if painful) look into your drinking habits. I did the same thing when I first started "getting real" with myself about it. Knowledge is power, and once you have the knowledge of the damage that alcohol is causing you, it will be much easier to walk away and never look back.

I quit all alcohol when I finally had the realization that drinking was only causing me unnecessary suffering. There was nothing fun about drinking anymore and I wondered if there really ever was. I personally got to the point where the only positive I could find about alcohol was the act of purchasing it. The anticipation of drinking was the only fun part. I was buying into the romantic idea of wine. Eventually even procuring the alcohol also led to suffering because when I would acquire it, I knew I would just want more. Another glass, another bottle, more more more…an endless pit of craving that could never be filled. When you start wanting and needing more alcohol is when all the horrible things start happening in your life. I decided to step off the path before it got really ugly.

To an outsider, I wasn't someone who you might think would even need to quit drinking as my life still looked very normal. I was a pretty "moderate" drinker. I had "controlled" my drinking for decades and took regular "breaks" from drinking all the time. I was just a regular yoga teaching mom who enjoyed having wine on the weekends. Most friends of mine were shocked when I stopped. They would say, "But you obviously aren't an alcoholic. Why stop?" I had never had a DUI, I didn't drink daily, no domestic violence charges or anything major, so why give up something that is such a part of society and so widely accepted.

You may read this book and think otherwise. You may decide that according to your standards I drank too much, or you may read it and think, "Wow, she didn't drink nearly as much as I drink." This is one of the reasons I stopped drinking. The slope is just way too slippery. The term "alcoholic" conjures up various images of hardcore drinkers who start vodka in the morning and can't hold down a job. Most people think alcoholics are those people with domestic violence issues, jail time, hospital visits etc… We all have preconceived ideas of how much drinking is too much and that view conveniently changes according to how much we are drinking. We take quizzes to see if we drink too much, we compare ourselves to others and how much they drink, we google how much is too much. Ultimately, we all tell ourselves we don't drink too much so we can continue on. We aren't in jail or in a gutter somewhere and we are just "social drinkers" so all is good, right? The reality is deep down we all know it's toxic. We know it's destructive, yet we keep doing it. There was definitely some place in me that completely knew drinking was a poor choice. One that I continued to make throughout my adult life. Drinking also took up way too much headspace for me. The energy I spent feeling guilty about drinking was not fun.

One day I was just done, and the facade was over. I no longer fell for the lie that alcohol leads to a fun filled life. My own reality told me otherwise. I decided to start listening to myself instead of society. Deep down I wanted to just be done with it, but for a long time some part of me couldn't give it up. I wish I had known what I know now, and I would have quit much sooner. I didn't realize it really was just a decision. I just needed to say-"No thanks, I don't drink" and it would be so. I thought it had to be this long, horrible grieving process where I no longer got to enjoy life. I had read several books and articles online about what an arduous journey it would be. That was the last thing I wanted. No one told me it could be more simple. I was a decision away from having my life back and I postponed it for so long.

What I have found is that giving up alcohol is not at all like I thought it would be. Every single thing about stopping has been positive for me. Since making the decision to cut alcohol out of my life, I feel liberated, empowered, energized, strong, smart, loving, happy and connected. Actually, I feel the exact opposite of how I felt when I drank. I am so thankful I made the decision to quit because I know how the drinking path ends and it doesn't end well. It's a bottomless pit that is never filled and I am grateful I am no longer a slave to its endless well. Thankfully, I was not chemically addicted to alcohol, as I quit before I got to that place. I am not a medical expert or an expert on addiction. I am someone who used to drink and made the decision to stop. I am sharing my personal story with others with the hope that it will be of benefit anyone who needs it.

This book can help you even if you are chemically addicted to alcohol. You can use the techniques I mention once you have received medical support. The key to quitting any habit that no longer serves you is to find what works for you. Some people have found success with AA, some with an online network of people. I never used either of those tools, so I cannot speak about them. My background is in yoga and meditation so a substantial part of my path to sobriety was to become fully dedicated to those disciplines. I finally decided to commit to a full-time yogic lifestyle instead of a part time one. This decision made all the difference.

PART ONE

THE PATH TO ALCOHOL

1

OPENING MY EYES TO THE POISON

For most of my adult life, I have been committed to a very healthy lifestyle. Before I became fully sober, I would exercise and eat super healthy during the week, only to then drink wine every weekend. I have always been very careful with my diet. I eat organic foods, I juice, participate in cleanses, drink my smoothies and take my vitamins. I don't use toxic chemicals in my house, yet I was regularly drinking the most toxic substance of all, Alcohol. I was sabotaging all of my health and spiritual efforts with regular consumption of wine.

Eventually, I started to realize yoga is about relationship. The relationship you have with yourself, with others and with all beings. Yoga is also about our relationship with the substances in our lives. The substances we choose to ingest on a daily basis. Because I have always been committed to leading a healthy lifestyle and it's just a part of who I am at this point, I always found it frustrating that I couldn't seem to end my relationship with alcohol. I had no problem giving up certain foods that were unhealthy, quitting smoking cigarettes and even smoking cannabis (which I really enjoyed and was also a major part of my life for a very long time). For some reason alcohol was different. I couldn't imagine never drinking wine again. I had been drinking since I was pretty much a child. A world without wine just felt strange. I kept telling myself the health benefits of a glass of red wine and justified it by mostly indulging on the weekends and always having "rules' that made me believe my drinking was under control. The problem was I really never just had just one glass. Most of the time it was much more than that, and of course with time things only got worse as they always do with alcohol. I felt like I was living two separate lives. I knew I wanted and needed to quit drinking but some part of me couldn't release it. Yoga is about freedom, but I never felt free even with all the practice I did over the years. I was still bound to alcohol in a big way. Now that I have stopped completely, I can say 100% that drinking was blocking my spiritual progression. The crazy thing is, rarely anyone talks about this.

I do have one memory of a wonderful teacher who I studied yoga philosophy and meditation with, giving me some advice regarding alcohol. It was 1999 and I was living in India for several months and doing some in depth studies with this particular teacher. He was giving me a Vedic astrology reading, and all of a sudden he became very serious and exclaimed, "Alcohol is destructive. You need to stop drinking." I cringed when he said this as I knew he was aware of the fact that I liked wine and drank it pretty regularly. I was in my twenties and even though I was passionate about yoga and had pretty much dedicated my life to it. I still loved my wine. Apparently, there was no fooling him and the jig was up. He knew I was not quite on the yogic path in a full way. I was ingesting a harmful substance and he didn't agree with it. I nodded and he continued with the reading. I have never forgotten this statement, even though at the time I just chalked it up to him being a very strict brahmin yogi. I assumed he had no idea what it was like to be in my shoes and a "little bit of drinking" wouldn't hurt me. Turns out I was completely wrong. How I wish I had listened to him and stopped drinking altogether when he gave me those pearls of wisdom. Fast forward 20 years later and I found myself on the path to having a major problem with alcohol. Now that I am living the sober life, I completely see why he was so blunt about it. For me personally, even just a slight attachment to drinking alcohol was impeding my spiritual progress in ways I couldn't see until I stopped drinking.

I used specific techniques to achieve sobriety. I have outlined these methods in this book. Primarily a meditation practice, healthy diet, positive mind techniques, connecting with nature and practicing mindfulness in all areas of life. I have kept it pretty simple and it has worked very well. So well in fact, that I haven't found giving up alcohol to be the torturous journey that so many speak about. The way I see it, the torturous life was the life I had that included alcohol. I don't think this is because I was any less psychologically addicted than most people (I drank throughout my entire adult life.) I think the difference is in how I perceived quitting, and this is all about how you train your mind. If you train your brain to view giving up alcohol as a negative experience, it will be a negative experience. I have perceived it as a positive decision since the day I quit, and so for me, the process has been positive. I started changing my negative mindset before I quit drinking, and this has made all the difference. Once I started feeling better, giving up alcohol was the next natural step. I think it would have been much harder had it been the other way around. I finally got happier (in my mind) and then I lost the desire to drink. The rest was just habit and getting rid of the habit is much easier than getting rid of the desire. Your mind is a powerful tool, and you can use it to serve or to harm. The choice is yours.

My hope is that this book will give insight to others who may be struggling with the same dilemma, whether you are a yogi or not. The choice to completely cut alcohol out of your life feels like a major one for most of us. This is primarily because it is so prevalent in our world today. It is so easy to just continue drinking, saying you will just do it casually or only on special occasions, but for many of us this doesn't work, and you don't realize it until you are in the throes of major self-destruction. The problem with "casually or sometimes" is that with alcohol it always turns into more because it is a drug. A drug that can destroy.

Society doesn't warn us about this destruction. In contrast to what my teacher in India told me, the advice I received from the rest of the world was that drinking is fine in moderation. This is a very dangerous message as we each have different ideas of what moderation is. It can be very tempting to change your view of what moderate is to suit your own drinking. I know I did this. First moderate was one or two glasses, then moderate turned out to be a bottle, but only on the weekends. Daily drinking was never moderate in my mind. We all have our little head games around this.

I have found it much easier just not to participate anymore. This frees up an enormous amount of energy to be spent on more productive habits. Even if you don't consider yourself to be a "spiritual" person, and enlightenment isn't a goal for you. If alcohol has its grip on you then it is blocking you from your best self. I have been amazed how much time and energy I find myself with now. Time that used to be spent, thinking about, planning, and strategizing my drinking. You might think you don't do this, and you probably won't notice until you stop drinking. Once you make the decision to say, "No thanks, I don't drink." A whole world opens up to you. One with bright mornings, better relationships, and a healthier body and mind. This isn't to say life will be perfect and you will no longer have problems. But those problems won't be enhanced by alcohol fueled poor decisions and drama. You will be amazed at the theatrics you have most likely created for yourself, whether it be unnecessary fights with loved ones, delusional problems you fabricated, or the guilt you constantly have. This drama takes so much of your precious mental energy.

Once you have this mental transformation, drinking no longer holds any appeal. My approach to an alcohol-free life is one about changing your mindset. Retraining your brain to think about alcohol in a different light. For me, once I realized I had been duped by the alcohol industry, I no longer bought into the idea that alcohol was some fun filled, life enhancing substance. I saw it for what it is. A toxic, destructive poison that leads to nothing but misery. Luckily, I had this realization before I was chemically addicted and drinking completely ruined my life like it has for so many others. I hope this book has found you at the perfect time and you too can quit and move on to a more fulfilling, happier existence. I have discovered that shifting my paradigm in regard to alcohol has made all the difference. My experience has proven that being sober and living life to the fullest is a great lifestyle and really is our birthright. The sober life is the complete opposite of a drunk, numb, hazy, and dull existence.

When you take off the drunk goggles, you will see life in a more vivid, beautiful way. There is no way you will want to go back to the boozy life. You will have such an impetus to stay sober.

~

When I started seriously considering "breaking up" with alcohol, I spent some time reading about others who had quit. I remember feeling weird even reading those types of books, almost like reading them meant I definitely had a problem. As soon as I would finish one of them on my kindle, I would delete it as I didn't want recommendations for more of the same genre. I realize now I felt shameful even just reading about addiction. I think this is because I knew I wasn't chemically addicted and not in need of rehab or anything, I just really wanted to quit drinking. I didn't understand at the time that you can decide to quit without being an alcoholic. This is a choice anyone can make. Society always makes it seem like everyone should drink as much as they can, for as long as they can, and then you have to stop once you become an "alcoholic." Almost like "ok now the fun is all over and you are in the club of people who can no longer drink." I felt like quitting before I was labeled an alcoholic would either give me the "alcoholic stigma" or just seemed like a strange decision considering I still had a free pass to drink. I knew I wasn't what society would consider a heavy drinker, but alcohol was causing so much negativity in my life, it seemed like a poor decision to keep imbibing.

I was drinking a lot of wine on the weekends and really didn't think it was fun anymore. I wondered if anyone else felt the same way. As it turns out, many people felt the same way. I read tragic stories of people overcoming horrible addiction and destruction. Their novels were brutally honest, some horrifying, and some even riveting. The one thing they all had in common though, was that as I read them, all I wanted to do was drink. I would sit down to read a book that I assumed would encourage me to stop drinking and midway through the second chapter I would be pouring a glass of wine. I think this happened because each story had detailed descriptions of drinking. Pouring the wine, watching it settle into the glass, that fuzzy feeling when it washes over you and you forget your troubles and on and on. It was as if all these people worked so very hard to stop drinking, yet they still craved it. The way they wrote made my mouth salivate for it. I wondered, "Are they still sober because it sure sounds like they love to drink? How can you stop something you love so much? Did they spend the rest of their lives miserable because they couldn't have their precious wine, vodka or whatever?" I now realize writing these memoirs was part of their healing. They needed to write as part of their process. As I now know, once you stop drinking, you do heal, and you have time to do all those wonderful things you never quite got around to doing.

The truth is we've all been duped into thinking alcohol is needed to have a good time in life. My story demonizes alcohol because I no longer find it glamorous at all. In fact, I don't think I ever did, I was just listening to what society told me to think.

2

IT'S A FAMILY AFFAIR

S ociety isn't the only place I was taught that drinking "is fun." My family held the same perspective. I officially started drinking alcohol as a young child. My parents would have dinner parties and I would toddle around taking sips of everyone's scotch and waters. The adults all laughed and thought I was precious. Yes, that's how it was in the 70's, at least at my house. I do think I got a taste for it though, as I didn't just take sips at one party. I have multiple memories of doing this. Mostly I think I did it for the laughs initially. It felt good to have the adults pay attention to me. Usually, they were just drinking and ignoring me. I learned at a young age, if you join in the fun, people will like you. Not much has changed in life. For many of us, part of the path to a life of drinking is growing up with parents who drink. Both of mine drank heavily and I'm convinced this is one reason they both died from cancer.

My dad was a "martini man," kind of like James Bond. He looked and acted the part. He was handsome, funny, smart, and kind. A class act of a man who could hold his liquor. I think I only saw him drunk once or twice but he drank daily. My mom was a character. She was well mannered, funny, smart, and brought a lot of light into the world (until she would start drinking). Mom was more of a "wine-o." She loved her white wine and would drink it by the gallons. I'm sure my dad got more drunk than I saw but I was only with him on the weekends as they divorced when I was three. Mom was my primary caretaker and she was drunk and stoned throughout my childhood. She worked hard and played hard. She had a full-time job and yet somehow always managed to have a home cooked dinner on the table. Other than working full time, her main hobby was drinking. I remember being so scared she was going to die. She would get looped out of her mind while on the couch listening to Barbara Streisand or Pink Floyd. I would sneak down and sit on the stairs and watch her, wondering why she seemed to have such a hard life and what did I do wrong to make her drink so much. Why did she hate her life and me? When she wasn't drinking, she was irritable and when she was drinking, she mostly raged. Really fun times. There were several instances when I threatened to tell my dad she was regularly smoking pot too. She would always remind me that if I told him I would have to go live at his house. This was in the eighties when cannabis was considered a "dangerous" drug. I knew my dad would not be ok with me living in a house with that going on. Even though alcohol was the drug that made her mean, not pot. As much as I secretly wanted to live with my dad and found that scenario appealing, I also really loved my mom and worried about her. I didn't want to leave her. My dad and stepmom had two children together. I had a half brother and sister whom I adored. They lived in a very nice home in Atlanta, but I didn't have my own room when I visited every weekend. I stayed in a guest room and always felt like a visitor in my own father's house. The thought of going to live with them made me anxious. I was also scared I would really miss my mom. So, I stayed with her and learned to keep her drugs and rages a secret. My dad had no clue about some of the things that happened to me because of my mom's drinking.

When you're a child you have no reference of what is normal behavior and what is not. You might have abuse going on, but it's just your life experience and all you know.

Especially when you grow up with parents who drink, you usually aren't allowed to have feelings about anything. With heavy drinkers, it's all about them. So, you stuff any weird feelings way way down and the one thing that helps them go away is drinking, Not only are you emulating what you have been taught you are supposed to do, you are also trying to numb yourself from your pain, so the cycle continues. As we all know alcohol abuse is often passed down in families. Some attribute this to alcoholism being a disease. Something you are born with. You don't get the free pass to drink all you want like everyone else. To me the jury is still out on this one. There is too much evidence that points to the fact that no one is immune to the risk of alcohol addiction. Alcohol is a drug just like heroin or crack. No one gets a free pass. The habits and choices you make decide your path more than your brain chemistry. You are not doomed to a life you have no control of.

Part of the argument about someone's predisposition to abuse alcohol is their environment. We see this over and over. People who grow up with people who drink become drinkers. Is this really just some defective brain chemistry? Or does it make more logical sense that the very people we look up to in the world and want to be like (our parents) drink all the time so we do too? It's just what we know. Kind of like following the religion your parents follow. If your parents are Jewish, you are raised Jewish. If your parents are Christian, you are raised Christian. If your parents are drinkers, you are most likely a drinker (unless you grew up with such extreme trauma caused by alcoholic parents, that you swore it off.) The difference is when you become an adult and you decide you don't agree with your parent's religion, you can change it, but if they have turned you into a drinker by initiating you into that "religion," chances are you are now addicted and changing your mind isn't as easy. If you really pause and think about it- how crazy is it that many of us were offered sips of alcohol from our parents?!

Did your parents offer you cocaine or crack? Probably not. Why is it considered normal and fun for parents to drink with their children? I certainly didn't want to pass my own addictions to my kid. The last thing I wanted to do was to push alcohol on him and have him end up hooked on something that would forever steal his power and ruin his life. I hated my own addiction. Why would I ever want to pass that along to him? I am still angry that this was done to me.

The question is- Do parents introduce their children to alcohol to justify their own drinking? I know at my house the adults waited around for happy hour like it was the second coming of Jesus. It was the highlight of the day. My sweet grandmother loved it so much, that when she lost her mind in her 70's, she would start asking at noon "when is happy hour?" I was raised hearing this constantly. Adults talking about happy hour, drinking time, cocktail hour, party time, etc... It seemed the adults in my life were never "happy" until happy hour. Why would I think any differently? All of my elders taught me alcohol was the key to "happiness." The sad thing is none of them were truly happy. They all dealt with depression and addiction throughout their lives, most of which was caused by their consumption of alcohol. They clung to this one hour of the day when they thought they could erase their troubles with a magic potion which was in fact a poison. And they did it day after day after day, never with a different result.

Some of us are introduced to more than just alcohol from our parents. My path to pot also started with my mom. I learned from a pro. My mom was the perfect country club wife while married to my dad, but when she left him, she kind of went wild.

My childhood was spent sniffing around the house for her dope. I was raised in the Reagan era when Nancy Reagan was telling the world how bad drugs were. Nancy had turned anyone under ten into a narc. Because of all the information I was bombarded with at school, I was constantly worried about my mom's drinking and marijuana consumption. I knew my mom smoked pot all the time. She would burn incense to cover up the smell, but I was smart enough to put two and two together and knew that when I smelled incense this meant she was toking it up. She and I fought about it constantly. I hated that she did drugs and I really hated it when she drank. At least with pot she was mellow. She wasn't a mellow drunk and as I mentioned, I was often the brunt of her rage. However, I truly believed if I left her and went to move in with my dad, she would die from drugs and alcohol. This left me with a very worrisome and lonely childhood. I spent most of my time outside. Nature was my refuge and to this day, being outside is where I find peace.

How about you? Reflect for a moment about your own childhood. It is important for us as we figure out where we are headed in life to take a look at where we have been. What was your childhood like? Did you grow up in a home with parents who drank regularly? Did both parents drink or just one? Was your childhood peaceful, chaotic, safe, or unstable? Try not to judge the experience as you remember it, just have an honest look. What ideas do you have about drinking alcohol that were formed early in life?

Drunk people are very scary to children and if you are consuming with them around, it is causing issues whether you are aware of it or not. You are also teaching them that drinking is the right way to deal with the stresses of life. Has it served you? Is this really what you want to model for your children? Do you want them to grow up and have an alcohol addiction? Do you want them to crave alcohol and/or drugs like you do? Can you truly say yes to any of those questions? I know I couldn't, and I still regret that I modeled such behavior. I am grateful that at some point I realized the negative impact it was having on my family and grateful my son was able to see me make the decision to quit. I talked in depth with him about my choices and regrets. I am so thankful I came to my senses and made these decisions while he is still a teenager.

A few years before my mom died, she was much more mellow in her drinking (due to illness.) During that end phase of her life we were able to have a more healthy and strong relationship. I often think of my mom and wish she would have had these same realizations about her relationship to alcohol. I honestly think she knew it was damaging but just couldn't kick it. Or it was just more important than everything and everyone else? This is what children think. When they so desperately want you to quit. They think you love the drug more than you love them and actually this is the message you are sending.

When you are in the throes of addiction, this is actually what happens. You cannot imagine being without your beloved drug. You will make excuses, blame everyone else, create rules to help others feel better about your habit, etc... You do all of this to postpone the inevitable fact that you must quit. What you don't realize is the postponing is what is causing all the suffering. If you would just make the decision and do it, you would eventually be free. I'm not saying it will be easy, but it will definitely be easier than the torture you are now experiencing. Wanting to quit but thinking you aren't able to is a terrible feeling. The only person making it hard is you. You are in charge of your life. Take back your power and do it. Let go of the toxic substances and feel free again.

3

THE TEENAGE & COLLEGE YEARS

Time moved on and as I approached my teenage years, I decided to join the club of drinkers. The real drinking started when I was 15. I almost started a year or two earlier as most of my girlfriends started drinking at age 13. I recall several slumber parties where they were all drinking and smoking but I held out. I had gone to a religious school in 7th grade and I was convinced all of my "partying friends" were going to Hell for their actions. I certainly didn't want to join them. The girls couldn't change my mind. Eventually it was a boy who initiated me into the world of weekend drinking.

It was the beginning of 10th grade, and I had started dating a blonde haired, blue eyed troublemaker. That's trouble with a capital T. His name was Shane, and he was a year older than me. Shane picked me up in his super slick, white Audi for our first date. When I got into the car, I noticed there was something in the floorboard. My foot bumped a four pack of wine coolers. "I'm going to teach you to drink," Shane said. Boy did he ever. We shared the wine coolers and I ended up throwing up out the window of his Audi that night and pretty much every other weekend night of tenth grade. Shane loved to drink and do other drugs. I was still scared of anything besides alcohol, so I never tried his weed or cocaine. The alcohol was strong and got me loaded enough each time we were on a "date." It seemed strange to me that I always vomited, and he didn't. I just kept thinking I needed to drink more to raise my tolerance to his level. I also started drinking with all those girlfriends of mine who had been drinking since we were 13. I finally felt like I was a part of their click. I was no longer the outcast who didn't "have fun." Just like when I was a young child, I received the message that to be a part of things and to have fun, I needed to drink. Maybe I could even make people laugh like I did when I was a little kid sipping those scotches. Alcohol made me feel more attractive and funny. Little did I know booze actually made me less attractive and less smart in the long run, but I was young and wild and free! Ignorance is after all totally bliss, right?

I continued to drink throughout high school. Usually spending my weekends not only puking out of Shane's car, but also hunched over some strange toilet at a party. Alcohol never quite agreed with me, but I kept at it as it's what we all had in common. I couldn't imagine the high school experience without it. I was a cheerleader and even though I was smart and could get B's and C's without studying, I could really have cared less about academics. Boys and parties were my thing. I wasn't really into health at the time and didn't exercise much except for cheering. My diet was crap and I also started smoking cigarettes. My mom had a special porch in our apartment just for smoking. I wanted to be like her and that's what she did. She smoked and drank wine. Just like with alcohol, I hated smoking at first as it made me so nauseous, but I kept at it until I was totally addicted. Eventually my mom started letting me have friends over to drink wine and smoke. She even joined us most of the time. I was 15 and drinking and smoking with my mom. As were my friends. Looking back, I realize how completely dysfunctional this was but at the time it seemed perfectly normal. I grew up hating it when my mom would drink, but once I joined her it was "fun." She wanted to hang out with me unlike before when I just seemed to be in her way. She liked my friends and acted like she was one of us. I again got the message that if I drank, I was loved and accepted. Talk about peer pressure.

Around the end of tenth grade, I added marijuana into the mix. I can't remember if it was my very first or second time smoking weed but one of those times was with my mom. The other time was in a basement at a party with some weird skeleton bong. My friends and I were hanging out with some guys in a band and a few other dudes from school. They put the weed in the bong, and it all seemed super creepy and dubious. Again, Nancy Reagan had been telling all of us how horrible it was. I remember feeling like a bad girl. I also remember it didn't affect me that much and I didn't see what all the fuss was about. Still, I wanted to know what the big deal was with cannabis. I knew my mom smoked pot all the time and I had started to become curious about it as many of my friends had tried it. I went to a small private school and about 1/3 of my ninth-grade class had already tried weed. Since It was obvious my mom loved it, I decided to ask her why. We had so many fights about it when I was young, and she obviously didn't care what I thought. I knew she must love it and alcohol even more than she loved me, as I had begged her to quit countless times. I just wanted a normal, sober mom. She resented me calling her on it all the time but as I had gotten older, I just conceded to the fact that this is what she did and that's the way it was. Well, you know the saying, "If you can't beat em, join em," this is kind of where I was with the situation. Peer pressure from my own mom. I knew she would welcome my intrigue with pot, and it would probably give us a bond. I realize this might sound fabulous to someone who smokes pot. You probably think it would have been great to get high with your parents. Actually, it was totally awkward and weird. I always hated how my mom acted when she was high and then when I got stoned with her it was even more dysfunctional and strange.

Mom and I were on a road trip to Asheville, North Carolina to visit my grandparents. I figured it was the perfect opportunity to broach the subject. I started telling her that all my friends were smoking marijuana and I was curious. She got a little smirk on her face and said, "Open the glove compartment." I opened it up and there was a fat joint. My mom then got an even bigger smirk and said, "Light it up." I totally froze. I was thinking, "Wait! What! I just wanted some info about the drug, I don't actually want to smoke it with you. You're my mom!" But as I said, I intuited it would bond us, so I lit it up and continued to get super baked with my mom. We pulled into my grandparents driveway about an hour later, red eyed and very high. My mom told me to go straight inside and pour a glass of wine so they would just think I had a wine buzz instead of a pot buzz. Seriously, my own mother was telling me to go drink. I was 15 years old. Is it any surprise I became a stoner and a drinker?

After that stoned road trip with my mom, I tried to avoid smoking pot with her very often as it was so weird and honestly at that point in time, I really didn't like cannabis very much as it made me paranoid. It wasn't until my twenties that I became a daily "wake and baker." I still preferred alcohol. So, I drank with my mom. We drank a lot and my friends continued to drink with us as well. My mom was the "cool mom." The one who let us underage drink at the house. She never let us drive and it was only on weekends, but other than that we could do what we wanted. All of my friends envied me, and they loved that they could talk to my mom about anything. Little did they know I envied them and the fact that they were being parented in a more traditional way. Like I said, I really wanted a sober mom, and I knew it was dysfunctional that my mom hung out with my friends and I while we drank. But she and I were getting along better, we didn't fight as much because I joined in on her habits. Now that I was a drinker, I really couldn't continue to ask her to stop. She had passed the torch to me. I was to carry on the family addictions. Sadly, this is what happens in a lot of families. Very often we mimic our parents. We follow their lifestyles and habits as this is what we know. By the time we realize it isn't a very happy existence, it is often a little late and we have our own addictions to now deal with.

Do you have children? If so, do you want this same kind of addictive lifestyle for your precious children or can you teach them to make different choices? Trust me it isn't going to work for you to ask your kids to do something you aren't doing. So if you can't retrain your brain to dislike alcohol and drugs for yourself, then think about your kids. You will have no regrets and it will be the best decision you have ever made for everyone involved. It would have been the happiest day of my life if my parents had made the decision to quit drinking. Instead, I ended up losing them both to cancer.

High school rolled along, and I continued to drink on the weekends. I then went away to college to get my degree in Elementary Education. Oddly enough, my first year of college was a phase of life where I decided to quit drinking. I know this sounds strange as Freshman year is typically the year of total debauchery for most kids, but I went to a Baptist college. My parents sent me there, not because we were Baptist, but because they thought I might actually study if I attended a nice conservative school. This actually was the idea of my high school counselor. She thought I might have a chance of thriving without so much temptation around. The plan worked (at least initially) as I fell for a nice southern Baptist boy who didn't drink or do drugs. Unlike my high school boyfriend who encouraged me to drink, this one despised alcohol. Because I was so boy crazy, I of course quit drinking while trying to please him. I didn't drink my entire freshman year and I actually didn't miss it. My boyfriend and I had a blast sober, it all seemed really healthy and normal. I was the happiest I had been in years and never thought I would drink again. It had been easy to quit, since I had only been a drinker for a couple of years. Sadly, it didn't stick.

I went to the beach that summer with my best friend. She and I always summered together. We would go to the beach with our respective families. We were two peas in a pod. Mostly what we had in common was smoking and drinking. My friend was dumbfounded that I had quit drinking, and she and my mom made it their mission to get me back into it. Both of them disliked my boyfriend (mostly because he didn't party). They said he was judgmental and aloof, but I knew they just felt weird around him because he didn't partake in drinking. My mom continued to point out his flaws. Going over and over what she didn't like about he and his "prudish teetotaling family." At the same time they continued to push alcohol on me, "just have a sip" they would say, "You used to be so much fun. Now you are so judgmental." I started to doubt everything. I gave in and started drinking again.

My boyfriend came to visit me a few weeks later and I broke up with him. It shocked him, broke his heart, and to be a honest mine too. I guess at the time I decided to choose alcohol over him. That was about 30 years ago and other than abstaining for nine months (in my thirties) when I was pregnant with my son, I continued throughout adulthood using alcohol and other drugs. I often wonder what my life would have been like if I had stuck with sobriety back then. Cutting out alcohol in college wasn't terribly hard, I had only been a drinker for 3 years. Quitting after having been a drinker for 35+ years was more mentally challenging. The choices we make truly decide the trajectory of our lives.

I went back to college after that summer and continued to drink. I probably didn't drink as much as a typical kid who attends a secular school. My college was religious, so my friends and I had to search out the parties. We didn't have peer pressure every night of the week. But still, I was usually drinking 3 out of 7 days a week. I was becoming kind of a "weekend warrior" drinker. I lived for the weekends and was setting up a pattern of alcohol being the "reward" to the end of a long week. I didn't realize it at the time, but this would become a pattern that clung to me throughout adulthood.

I think about my friends who did drink daily in college, were they also setting up drinking patterns for life? I guess "higher education" takes on a whole new meaning. During my college years, I had a friend who worked in a restaurant most nights after her classes. She would take shots and drink liquor with her coworkers after her shift. She would come back to the dorm pretty loaded. When I reconnected with her 20 years later, she was still drinking vodka daily and joked about being a functioning alcoholic.

How many of us start these patterns when we are such young adults? Giving in to the peer pressure of a boozy college or a toxic/alcohol fused work environment. We don't realize at the time we are creating a life that will revolve around booze. Society expects college kids to party, we are encouraged to "let loose" with our peers. No one feels bad about being drunk all the time in college as it's just what kids do. So, what happens after college once you have already become addicted and it's time to face the real world?

4

POTHEADS

For me the "real world" meant turning to pot instead of booze. After graduating from college, I met my first husband, Bud. Bud was a full-on hippie. Maybe you guessed it from his name. In fact, when I met him, he had just gotten out of jail for growing the real "kind bud." This was the early 90's when "kind bud" was a rarity. He knew how to grow it and he made a lot of money selling it. I was intrigued. Bud was different from the guys at my college. They seemed so boring compared to what he was up to. Instead of studying, he was riding around on racing motorcycles and slinging weed. It all seemed so dangerous and thrilling. I quickly got caught up in his world and gave up sorority life for something that seemed more fun. Eventually Bud and I got married. We had a beautiful southern wedding, and we shared a life together for several years.

A life that was a bit hazy due to all the pot we smoked. I actually became more of a stoner than drinker in my 20's and 30's. Bud had cannabis around all the time, so naturally I started smoking it more and more. This love of weed stayed with me throughout most of my adult life and I often used it when I wanted to "cut back" on drinking. Pot just seemed healthier and didn't have so many negative side effects. I also started to discover yoga around that time. I justified using cannabis regularly because in some yoga circles marijuana is widely accepted. There is quite a history surrounding cannabis and the Hindu god Shiva. Somehow it just seemed more acceptable since it is an herb and much less damaging than alcohol. I still didn't like the fact that I was addicted to something, even if only psychologically. At my core, I knew yoga and meditation could help me find more balance, if I could only give up all the other distractions. But I wasn't ready.

Bud did help me quit the terrible habit of cigarettes. Even though he smoked loads of pot, he had quit smoking tobacco. His mother was dying of emphysema and this gave him the motivation to quit. My own father had throat cancer at the time and even had his larynx removed. I knew I should quit but I was totally addicted. Bud decided to help me. Since he used to grow weed, he had all these extra leaves. He would roll them for me like cigarettes and I would smoke those instead of tobacco. It worked! After about 8 years of smoking daily, I quit. I remember I still wanted cigarettes for about a year, especially when I would drink. Eventually the desire disappeared. I always used to tell myself if I can quit smoking, I can quit anything. I would remind myself that I could quit drinking any time I wanted to. The problem was I never wanted to. It is so easy to say you can "take it or leave it" when you never try and leave it. I wouldn't let alcohol go until decades later.

Bud and I continued to smoke pot during the week and drink only on weekends. Being a weekend drinker worked for me as I could pretend I didn't have any major issues with alcohol. The problem I had, and most weekend drinkers have (even if they lie to themselves) is that because you only drink on the weekends and you "don't have a problem", you need to pack all of your drinking into 2 or 3 days. You tell yourself you deserve more since you don't drink every night. Why not have another glass (or another four glasses)? Sometimes you bend the rules and tell yourself you will start the weekend on Thursday this week and quit on Saturday. Also, there is often a holiday or special occasion during the week which becomes an extra drinking day. Tuesday might be that extra day if you've had a bad day. "You deserve it." You look forward to the weekends with a little too much enthusiasm because you know you will drink. Still, you tell yourself alcohol doesn't have a grip on you. The reality is you are drinking 3-4 days per week (most weeks) as there is always a celebration or holiday to be found. Not to mention vacations which allow you to throw all rules out the window. So ultimately the "weekend drinker" status is a facade and a joke. You are still a heavy drinker and are just ignoring this fact. Yes, it might take you longer to become a full-blown alcoholic (whatever that looks like to you) but the day will come when it doesn't matter that it is just weekends when your life feels out of control. When you can't stop at one or two drinks, when you wake up regretting things you said or did, when your children look at you with disappointment every weekend when you start pouring that first drink, when you can't remember things from the previous night, when you wake up in the night with a pounding head and a sad, embarrassed spirit. The list is endless of the ways alcohol is destroying what could be a happy life just because you want a "fun" weekend. There will come a day when you finally admit this is no longer "fun" and you want your life back. If you don't stop completely, you may eventually find your entire world revolving around when you get to drink next. The parts in between just become the boring moments that you just get through until your next drink. This is when most people start drinking daily. Why wait until the weekend they say? "I'll just have some wine with dinner."

Would you consider someone who does cocaine every day addicted? Even if they just did a little? What about if they only did it on the weekends? Addicted? If you don't think they are addicted, at what point are they? When they can't get out of bed without it? Well, this is what happens with alcohol too, it just takes longer for most people. I guess in our society this is when someone would be labeled a "real alcoholic," when they need vodka in the morning, or they can't function. Do you want to get to that point before you stop? I sure didn't. Do you think anyone ever wants to be in that position? I doubt those people thought they would end up there as they had their glass of wine, then bottle of wine, then two bottles, then switched to something harder. How can any of us think we are stronger than those who end up in that place? They were ingesting the same exact drug.

The main reason I was only a weekend drinker with Bud is because he thought if we drank daily it would mean we were addicted to alcohol. He didn't want to become an alcoholic and I certainly didn't either. I didn't understand his way of thinking though, as this meant most of my family and friends were alcoholics in his mind. Thank god I didn't drink all the time or he would have meant me too (my self image was so important). His point was that people who ingest a drug daily must be addicted, why else would they do it. You may say, "Because they want to, there is nothing wrong with that." I remember thinking the same thing. Aren't people only addicted if they turn mean, have domestic violence issues, or start missing work? Obviously, Bud and I were mentally addicted to pot as we smoked that daily, but it didn't cause the issues that we thought drinking daily would eventually cause. Pot just made us mellow.

There IS an addiction if you are ingesting alcohol daily as it is a drug and eventually it will control you. NO ONE is immune to this. If you aren't addicted, why do it? It's like playing with fire. Eventually you will get burned. This business of calling certain people alcoholics and everyone else gets a free pass to drink all the time is ridiculous. We need to be done with these labels and realize that anyone who drinks can become addicted. It is just a matter of when. Sure your environment and genetics play a part in it (mine sure did). But don't kid yourself into thinking because your parents weren't heavy drinkers that you won't become one. A drug is a drug, and its job is to eventually make you a slave.

Because I kept up the habit of smoking cannabis regularly, I always used it as my "back up" drug. In my late teens and early twenties, I could still tell myself I was a "social" drinker. I really liked to drink but didn't have the pangs of guilt about it yet. I did have a voice in the back of my head that told myself I probably liked it a little too much, but I would just drown that voice out with more wine.

When I hit my mid-twenties, I started noticing myself craving wine more than just on the weekends. I didn't want to become a daily drinker, so I started smoking massive amounts of weed. I was definitely stoned more often than I was sober. Since I waked and baked I actually think I was just stoned all the time (except maybe for a few hours before I taught my yoga classes as I had a strict rule for myself about not teaching stoned.) I was so proud that I still only drank alcohol on the weekends. Bud and I would start drinking on Friday nights and continue throughout the weekend. Starting over on Mondays back to just pot. We typically didn't day drink, but we were partying until we were loaded every Friday, Saturday, and sometimes Sunday nights. The pot took the edge off during the rest of the week when wouldn't drink any alcohol. I also took speed on the weekends as Bud had a prescription for an ADHD medicine. I liked the pills more than he did and I would take them all weekend. I loved how they curbed my appetite and gave me energy (little did I know speed is one of the most evil drugs on the planet. I would have to deal with that addiction later in life). I liked how it made me feel and I would hardly eat all weekend. We would just drink and smoke pot. By Monday morning I would look emaciated and exhausted only to start the whole process over again the next weekend. Even just writing those words make me exhausted. It was a horrible cycle and a terrible way to live but it was my reality and all I knew at that point in life.

The blessing was that I had found yoga and was a serious yoga practitioner during that time and had been since I was 25. Gradually the more yoga I did the less interested I was in getting stoned. I started to feel pretty good in general and found myself saying no to weed more and more often. Getting stoned together was one of the main things Bud and I had in common. When I started to lose interest in smoking out all the time, our marriage suffered, and we started to grow apart. Even though I was toking the bong less and less, I still never said no to wine on the weekends. A shift happened and the less pot I smoked, the more I wanted to drink. The cannabis was curbing my urge to drink and when I started tapering off the ganja my desire for alcohol started to creep up on me. At that juncture in my life, I realized alcohol was the one drug I wasn't willing to let go of.

I went back to pot a few years later when I was having issues around alcohol and it curbed the urges for me just like it had done before. It was definitely my crutch. Pot was the drug that kept me from drinking too much. I continued to tell myself weed was ok as it was from the earth and even the sadhus (spiritual people) in India smoked it. I do believe (and statistics will back me up) that cannabis is far less destructive than alcohol. I also think it is more beneficial for certain issues than most pharmaceutical drugs on the market today. However, I eventually found marijuana to be an obstacle for my spiritual practices instead of an aid. When I would meditate stoned it was so "easy" and felt like total bliss. Now that I am sober, I realize it was a kind of fake samadhi. Pot gave me a false sense of bliss. Meditation without the aid of cannabis is a completely different experience. I couldn't realize any of this until I finally released all drugs and alcohol from my life. The sense of freedom this gives is better than any "high" I was receiving from drugs that would eventually dissipate, leaving me back at ground zero ready to start the cycle all over again. To end the addictions and discontinue this self-inflicted type of suffering, I chose to say goodbye to all of it.

Obviously, life is full of suffering and we can't eradicate it. What we can do is mindfully make choices that don't add unnecessary suffering to ourselves and others. This is one way giving up drugs and alcohol became a kind of spiritual practice for me. I started to realize if I truly loved myself and others, saying goodbye to drugs would lead to more contentment and happiness than the drug/alcohol journey. I had definitely been on the path of using external substances to find happiness, and I was anything but happy. I had taken the "breaks," made the rules around my drinking, and tried to put all my drug and alcohol abuse into neat and tidy boxes. This just didn't work, because at the end of the day, the drugs and alcohol were still in control and blocking me from my potential. Once I was able to fully release the grip of all of it, I was free.

5

ONE OF THE OLD SCHOOL YOGIS

I started yoga in the mid 90's after I graduated college. This was before yoga was a craze in America. In those days yoga wasn't considered very hip and was still a thing only crunchy/granola types did. I was quite the hippy girl back then (actually more of a hippy princess with my "southern girl" upbringing) but still, I was drawn to all things natural and organic. This included yoga. My dad had died the previous year and I had become a runner while trying to deal with my despair. Dad was my hero and losing him was the worst thing that had ever happened to me. A friend recommended yoga and I thought I would give it a try. My mom had dabbled with yoga and dance when I was a kid and I remembered doing some of the poses with her. I had also done ballet, tap, jazz, and gymnastics as a child and had always been quite flexible. Running was starting to make me a little bit stiff. I thought maybe this yoga stuff would help. I was also teaching elementary school at the time and really needed an outlet to help destress. My friend told me the teacher was an older lady and really sweet, I figured it couldn't be that bad.

I was still smoking a lot of pot, but I decided not to go to my first yoga class stoned. I got high before running but that was solo, I didn't want to get paranoid or feel weird around people during my first class. I walked in and was greeted by a very kind, gray haired lady. She had on a white "Yoga For Life" t-shirt with purple leggings and she was super toned and lanky. Her name was Mary Lou Buck and she was teaching a form of yoga called Kripalu Yoga in the basement of a Baptist Church (this was before yoga studios were really a thing in North Carolina.) Although the basement was dark and a bit weird, she had great energy and I instantly felt more calm in her presence. She was so sweet and welcoming.

She started the class by ringing some bells and then she put on some New Age kind of music. She continued to contort herself into shapes and asked us to follow along. From the instant the class started I was at ease. There was something so familiar about yoga, it was like coming home to myself. Before I tried yoga, any other exercise I participated in usually involved having a goal. I would do the activity to get fit or lose weight. Yoga was different, it felt good and effortless. My spirit was even happy. I remember thinking during that first class, "I'm going to teach yoga one day." I don't know why or how I knew it, but I did. I had found my calling.

Mary Lou continued to be my dear yoga teacher for several years. She was so loving and encouraging. I felt very lucky to have her as a teacher. I attended her classes religiously as I couldn't get enough. I was instantly a yoga zealot. Yoga completely overtook my life. I read and studied everything I could on the subject. I became a vegetarian and later a vegan and just cleaned up my life in general. Except for pot and alcohol, I wasn't ready to give those up. Weed kind of went with yoga anyway, so I didn't see a problem with it as long as I didn't go to class high. After about a year of daily practice, Mary Lou encouraged me to go to the Kripalu Center and get my teaching certification. I followed her advice and completed their month-long teacher training program. I came back to North Carolina a certified yoga teacher. I was eager and ready to teach at the new yoga studio Mary Lou had opened. In the interim Bryan Kest had visited NC and done a workshop on power yoga. I fell in love with this form of yoga as I had never experienced anything like it. Bryan was an amazing teacher, super charismatic and full of knowledge. I continued to study with him through workshops he would bring to different cities. Once I was certified to teach, I wanted to teach power yoga as it was now my main practice. I started teaching it at Mary Lou's studio and it was a huge hit! People loved it and somehow, they loved me even though I was a brand new teacher. Looking back, I now realize what they loved was my passion for the practice as I had very little knowledge of actual yoga. I had only been practicing for a year and I was 25 years old teaching people who were much older than me and who had been practicing yoga for a very long time. They didn't care that I was a new practitioner. They were the most supportive and loving group. Things were flowing so well, I felt I had truly found my dharma. I couldn't believe I was being paid to do something I loved so much. Life was good.

I remember receiving a letter from a precious couple who attended my yoga classes in Charlotte. They wrote to tell me how my classes were helping them on their road to recovery. They both had been severe addicts. They didn't know I was also using pot and alcohol. As I said, I was very careful not to smoke pot before I taught yoga. I had a strict rule that I would only smoke weed in the morning if I had to teach that night. What a guru I was.

Still my life path was rolling along in a positive way. Sadly, Bud was having a different experience. He was part of a startup company that was closing, so he was ready to move and make a change. I was torn as things were going so well for me in North Carolina. I was building my classes, loved the people who attended, loved my own yoga teacher and was really happy with what I was doing. I also loved my husband and hated his suffering and understood his need for change. We decided to take an extended trip to India and Nepal and then move to Colorado. I had met Pattabhi Jois at a workshop in Boulder, CO and I wanted to learn more about this Ashtanga

Yoga practice. We packed up our life and moved on. That first trip to India changed my life on so many levels.

After India, the last leg of our journey was spent trekking in the Himalayas. We then we returned to the United States and moved to Breckenridge, Colorado. Bud had a twin brother named Fred who lived in Breck. We wanted to live closer to him and it all seemed like the perfect plan for us after India. I had plans to open my own yoga studio there. As time moved on, it turns out life had other ideas for us.

I had started driving to Boulder every weekend to study and practice yoga with Richard Freeman. I was blown away with Richard's teachings. He presented yoga in a way I had never experienced, and I was eager to learn more from him. Little did I know at the time, Richard would become the most influential teacher of my life. I was tired of making the drive to Boulder from Breckenridge and wanted to live closer to Richard's studio, so Bud and I moved to Denver. Our marriage dissolved shortly after we moved. I continued to practice at Richard's studio, The Yoga Workshop. This studio became my second home.

During that same period, many changes happened in my life. I met my current husband Gray. Gray was also a yogi and a meditator. We were the perfect match. We shared a love of all things philosophical and yogic. We fell for each other quickly and married a few years later. Gray was so kind to me and he was sober. He didn't drink or smoke pot and was just really an all-around decent guy. We practiced yoga and meditation together and I continued to imbibe on the weekends. Gray didn't love that I was a drinker since he had already realized alcohol was a waste of time, but I told him I enjoyed wine and he would have to learn to deal with it. I had quit drinking for a guy once and I wasn't going to do it again. Alcohol had become too important to me. Gray and I eventually moved to Louisville, CO and ended up living there for 16 years. I continued studying and practicing with Richard, and eventually taught as his studio for many years. I will forever be grateful for those years of study, practice, and teaching at the Yoga Workshop. I view that time as a highlight of my life. The knowledge, kindness, and love I received from Richard, his wife Mary, and all of the yogis in that community forever changed me. It was a special time, and I am so fortunate to have been a part of it all.

The crazy thing is, regardless of all the amazing teachers, all the meditation and yoga, all the moments of bliss and health. I still wouldn't let alcohol go. It was the one constant. Like a chain around my neck, it kept me from truly being free. I was starting to become more of a slave to it but continued to tell myself - "There was no problem in sometimes drinking." "Everyone else does it." "Others do it more than me," "It's just a little."" Everyone needs to let loose sometimes." "I don't need to be so uptight." "There are worse things than a little bit of wine." The list is endless in the ways I would talk myself out of thinking I had any kind of problem with alcohol. But deep down I knew. I knew I liked and looked forward to "happy hour" a bit too much. Drinking had slowly, over a long time become a part of who I was. I didn't know who to be without it.

~

Time rolled on and Gray and I were blessed with a beautiful baby boy. We named him Haven and he is the light of my life. When I became his mother, it forever changed me. Like most moms, I had such high ideas of the mother I wanted to be. I had many horrible memories of my mom and how she acted when she drank, and I definitely didn't want to follow in her footsteps. My mom was a special person and I loved her dearly. I of course have positive memories of her love, kindness and special way of being. Sadly though, I mostly I remember her drinking. Drinking always seemed to be the most important thing to her. I didn't want my son to have this same experience. I wanted to do things differently. I wanted to be there for him in every way possible. I never wanted to rage at him and have him feel the fear that I grew up with. The fear that comes with having a parent who is out of control. I actually did a good job of this as I had a husband who would get the brunt of any emotional outbursts I would have due to imbibing. My own drinking was much more controlled than my mother's and I didn't rage. Still, I think even with moderate drinking, I wasn't the mother I could have been had I been sober all those years. If only I had quit earlier. Even though I don't believe in wasting energy with regrets, I will always regret this. Missing any moments of my life (especially those with my son) because of a wine buzz, makes me really sad. As drinkers, especially if we aren't raging alcoholics, we lie to ourselves. We tell ourselves a little wine (one bottle) is ok, mommy needs to take the edge off, all moms do it, we are supposed to do it, it's normal, all my friends drink, it's fun, it makes me a hip mom, etc…

Thankfully, I started motherhood off on the right foot. I of course didn't drink or smoke pot throughout my entire pregnancy. I remember when I went to the hospital with early labor pains, they told me to "go home, take a bath and pour a glass of wine." I was stunned. "But I'm still pregnant!" "No worries, you are at the very end of your pregnancy, one glass won't hurt, and it will help you relax." I couldn't believe it! They were telling me to drink. Hooray! My life without wine is over. On to motherhood! Then I was worried about how I could drink and still nurse like I wanted to. I could "pump and dump" or so I had heard. All would be ok, and I could mommy with a little help from alcohol, just like everyone else. I was about to have my beautiful baby and I could get back to drinking. How strange society was telling me to drink again as I entered motherhood instead of encouraging me to enjoy being with my newborn and the natural bliss that comes with that.

I am in no way blaming anyone else for my decisions, but I think it is important to notice the pattern here. Alcohol is constantly pushed on all of us. Our parents, our friends, movies, television shows, commercials, social media, magazines, newspapers. We cannot escape it and eventually it wears you down. It seems much easier to concede and just do what everyone else is doing even when your gut knows it is unhealthy.

After that glass of wine when I was sent home from the hospital, I really didn't drink much during the baby years as I found pumping and dumping to be a pain. I was blissfully in love with my baby and really not craving alcohol since I had quit during pregnancy. I nursed my son for three years.

Once I stopped nursing, I upped my drinking. For the first time in my life, I was drinking more than just on the weekends. Wine was definitely my crutch or little treat at the end of the day with a toddler. What I didn't realize at the time is that the wine wasn't actually a crutch but made mommying much harder. The depression, anxiety, and mood swings caused by the alcohol were not in fact "fun." The problem is society continued to tell me I should drink. Once again, the pressure to do what everyone else is doing played a part in my decision making. In the early 2000's when my son was born, it wasn't as much of a "mommy drinking culture" as it is now, but still it was there. My mommy friends would tell me how a glass of wine at the end of the day is like a "little treat" and makes evenings so much easier. My own mom would come over and suggest we open a bottle to help "us" relax.

Not only was I drinking more than ever, I also started using pharmaceutical drugs. I remembered how much I liked taking my ex-husband's ADHD medicine. I loved the extra energy, and I knew it would help me take off the weight I gained during pregnancy. I figured it would be the perfect "mommy's little helper" during the toddler years. Instead of turning to yoga and meditation to help me destress and gain energy, I turned to drugs. This time period was one of the worst stages of my life. I like to refer to this as, the "Drugstore Cowgirl Phase."

6

DRUGSTORE COWGIRL

Here is how I became a "Drugstore Cowgirl":
I looked up ADHD symptoms and set up an appointment with a shrink who specialized in attention deficit disorder. I did have most of the symptoms anyway, but I am quite positive a meditation practice would have helped me. My goal wasn't to stop attention deficit symptoms, it was to get high, gain energy, and lose my baby weight. I had never been to a shrink until I decided to search one out to get speed. My plan worked and I entered the toxic world of Big Pharma. The doctor diagnosed me with Attention Deficit Hyperactivity Disorder, and I was prescribed speed. When I had taken my ex-husband's speed recreationally, I only took it on the weekends to party. I had never taken it daily. Once I started taking it regularly I felt invincible. I could get everything done (and then some). I was uplifted and focused, got super thin, and even felt smarter. The perfect drug, right? WRONG. This drug turned out to be the most evil thing I have ever put into my body (besides alcohol) and I was addicted to it for two years. My body became emaciated, my mind paranoid, and my relationships suffered greatly.

This is how it went for me: First he prescribed the speed, then I needed a relaxation medication to combat the anxiety caused by the speed. Then, a new speed because the one I was on was no longer working, then a time release one, then an antidepressant (the first of many) because I eventually wasn't happy once the newness of the drug wore off. I refused sleeping pills even though the doctor suggested I take them along with everything else. I had speed, anti-anxiety, and anti-depressant drugs running through my veins. All the while I was also drinking loads of alcohol as the pills made me want to drink like I had never before. There was an unknown craving for alcohol to counter all the pills. Looking back, it's a wonder I didn't die from all this. I rarely ate and I barely slept. This combination made me nuts and I feel lucky I didn't die or end up in a mental ward.

During this insane phase, my mom received a lung cancer diagnosis. This was devastating to all of us. As dysfunctional as our relationship was, my mom was my best friend. I couldn't imagine life without her, and I went into a deep depression. My son was a preschooler at the time, and I was also now the primary caretaker for my dying mother. Doing all of her shopping, cleaning, emotional support, etc… I was a full-time yoga teacher and was practicing, teaching daily, and expending a tremendous amount of energy holding up a strong mask about what was really going on in my life. This was a heart wrenching time, and my husband stuck it out with me through it all. Talk about some dark secrets. I still don't know how I taught classes and appeared so centered when on the inside I was a wreck. I was like many other moms. Trying to do it all with the help of some very toxic substances that only made everything worse. I am grateful that I survived this period of my life and emerged with my family intact.

Eventually my mom died. I went into an even deeper depression and it was at this point that I decided I needed to stop all the medication. The pills were making everything worse. In 1 1/2 years, I had gone from never having taken any kind of pharmaceutical drugs (other than the brief time with my ex) to being completely dependent upon pills. I had zero natural energy. I had to make a change. My husband helped me by hiding the medications, and administering them in a very specific way. This allowed me to taper off. The shrink was no help and just kept writing prescriptions. He even tried to drop me as a patient when he realized I was addicted to all the pills he had prescribed (duh). At my lowest point he was going to just bail on me. He was not supportive at all. Instead of going to a hospital or rehab, I detoxed myself from all the pills at home with the help of my husband. It was excruciatingly painful, and the time frame is still quite a blur, but I did it. To this day I can barely even take an aspirin as I don't like putting any kind of pill into my body. The pharmaceutical merry go round is terrible and no one can take you off the ride except yourself. They will never stop taking your money or your life. I can't say I recommend doing it at home. It was probably very dangerous to my health and I'm lucky I didn't die. I had no clue what I was doing, I just knew my life was better before I started down the pill road and I wanted my spirit back.

I was on the couch for about a year. I watched tv with my son, baked banana bread, and just tried to rest. I literally had gotten to the point where I couldn't function without the medicine. Especially the speed as my body was so used to running at such a high level on fake energy. I had to take a break from teaching. My own yoga practice suffered as I had no stamina. I was a total mess, but I was getting clean (except for alcohol.) I wouldn't give that up and was still drinking wine. At some point I started teaching yoga again and this got me out of the house. I was still depressed without the fake energy pumping into me, but I figured I could at least go back to my yoga practice and see if it would help me find some balance. The problem was I had gone from having a 2+ hour practice which included practicing the 3rd and 4th series of Ashtanga Yoga to barely being able to move my body. I felt heavy, lazy, and dull, but at least it was "me" and not a bunch of pills coursing through my system. Learning to navigate in this new body and mind was a challenge but I was starting to feel more authentic, except for the drinking. Alcohol seemed to be the one vice I just couldn't give up. "Maybe one day" I would say to myself, "but not today." In my heart I knew I needed to quit.

My higher self knew that all the happiness I desired wasn't in a bottle but would flourish when I gave up all the wine. I didn't listen to my higher self though. I continued to tell myself that alcohol was a crutch. A crutch to survive this life. I didn't realize at the time that meditation was a much better tool. I had received glimpses of this while on retreats. I participated in several month-long yoga retreats with hours of sitting and I always felt amazing. Then I would get home and my urge to meditate would dwindle. Practicing asana felt more accessible. Meditation seemed so boring even though it felt good. I would get a consistent practice going and then something would always interrupt. Getting sick or taking a trip, and then I would just quit my daily sitting. I had practiced asana for decades, but meditation was always "on and off" for me. There is a saying, "Meditate don't medicate" and I couldn't agree more as I have lived it.

I am almost 100% positive, if you are reading this book, alcohol is probably not the only drug you use. You are most likely also taking pills. Thanks to our trusty society of pill pushers. No judgment and please know that I realize there are people who need prescription medication. People with severe depression, mental disorders and sickness. I am not referring to those people in this chapter. I am talking about your average person who goes to the doctor complaining of lack of focus or a bit of sadness or some trouble sleeping. Many issues that can completely be taken care of with a proper diet and some exercise. Just about every person I know who takes ADHD medication is addicted to what it does to their weight and how productive they think it makes them. Many of them could actually care less about their ability to focus. Also, if you truly feel you have an attention deficit issue. Meditate every single day for a year and watch your ability to focus improve tremendously.

Once you start the pill popping it isn't going to end well. The answer to your happiness is not in the latest pill your doctor is pushing. Or in that bottle of wine in your refrigerator. I personally believe Big Pharma has taken over. Millions of people are over medicated, and this is causing so much unnecessary suffering. I suffered in silence. Only my husband knew what was going on. Not my mother, my yoga teachers, my siblings, my closest friends or anyone. Once I started talking about it (years later) to friends, several of them said they were experiencing the same scenario. I started to understand that my story is not uncommon and sadly maybe even the new normal.

Now before you throw this book against the wall and think I am being super judgmental about everything. Please remember I have been down this path. I know how it works. You feel a bit sad and the doctor gives you a "low dose" of something to take the edge off. Then that causes sleepless nights, so then you need a pill to help you sleep. Then you can't quite get up from your slumber, so your doc prescribes some speed. The speed makes you edgy, so you need something for the anxiety, along comes the relaxation medication, and on and on and on. Along with all this pill popping you are drinking more than ever before because guess what…some of these pills make you actually crave alcohol like never before. You also think the alcohol eases the anxiety you now feel all the time, so the cycle continues. More pills, more alcohol, more pills, more alcohol. Plus, the super dangerous part of all of this is that certain drugs (speed in particular) masks how drunk you are, so you can drink copious amounts of alcohol. Another recipe for disaster.

Make the decision to hop of the pharmaceutical merry-go-round. You can stop just like I did. You can replace pills with healthier choices. You can use many of the techniques in this book while you wean yourself off slowly. You might need to do this before you can fully let go of alcohol. The pills might be making your alcohol cravings worse. I am not a doctor and am not making a medical recommendation to you. Talk to your own doctor about making any changes. Do your research though and don't trust a doctor who is constantly pushing the latest pills on you. Find a good doctor. One who listens to you and helps you take a healthy route to wellness. Unless you have been diagnosed with a severe mental illness, there are more healthy ways to live than being caught in the pill loop.

Once I finally hopped off the pill train, I slowly started to get back to myself. I began to have more energy, started to practice yoga and meditation again, and just felt all around better. I was still a bit depressed and wondered if cannabis would help. Pot had become legal in Colorado. I hadn't smoked in several years, but since it was now legal, I was curious. I also thought I still needed drugs. Could weed help my depression? I didn't realize at the time; my depression was most likely caused by regular consumption of wine. I still hadn't said goodbye to alcohol yet and was using all my dumb rules to pretend alcohol wasn't important to me. I was trying to control it by only drinking sometimes, weekends, just a certain amount etc…it was pretty exhausting, but I still couldn't imagine life without it. I thought pot might be fun to revisit. I decided to go to a dispensary and see what all the fuss was about.

I was like a kid in a candy store. Weed became my drug of choice again and I continued to check out just about every dispensary in Boulder. I thought it was amazing that a drug I had enjoyed years ago was finally legal. For a while it really helped curb my desire for alcohol. I cut back on my drinking again. I had replaced all the prescriptions and alcohol with cannabis. I was smoking pot 24/7. This lasted for a while and then eventually the alcohol crept back into my life. I was smoking pot daily and drinking on the weekends (just like I had done before.) The pot only kept the drinking at bay for so long. Eventually I stopped smoking pot (which was easy), but I didn't stop drinking at that point. Alcohol was the last drug to go for me.

7

THE SEARCH FOR HAPPINESS IN EUROPE

Like most people, I have constantly been on the quest for happiness. 20+ years of yoga, countless green smoothies, vegan diets, plenty of friends, lovers, and money. Multiple things to be grateful for and yet still I continued to be mostly unhappy. Also like many people, I tried to fill this aching, unhappy hole with alcohol, drugs, and sometimes crappy food (on top of all the healthy habits I had). I remember even as a child I was constantly saying I was bored (unhappy about it) and looking for things to do. As I got older, drinking alcohol is how I dealt with boredom. My higher self knew that occupying those boring times with activities like yoga and meditation would give me more contentment and happiness than drinking but drinking just seemed easier. Just open the bottle and poof, it calmed me down. This is what the alcohol industry wanted me to think. This is what I had been taught from society and from my family. However, once I started really examining my thoughts when I drank, I realized I was anything but calm after the first 10 minutes or so. The residue from drinking was sadness not contentment.

About two years before I decided to quit drinking for good, I had given up all the pills and the pot. I was still drinking every weekend and I felt bloated, depressed, anxious, and unfocused. I really started noticing this when I would drink alone. Because my husband isn't really a drinker, I started buying those little boxes of wine that are equivalent to about 3 glasses. I used to tell my husband that the box was mislabeled and there were actually only about 2 glasses at the most. Again, I was justifying my drinking and two glasses sounded better than 3. I really wanted to buy regular bottles of wine and sometimes I did, but in my effort to "control" my drinking, I mostly stuck with the tiny 500 ml black box of Cabernet on the weekends. One box on Friday and one on Saturday. When I started to really examine how I was feeling when I drank, I noticed after about the first glass, I no longer felt the "happy rush." I realized it was more the anticipation and the idea of relaxing with wine than the actual act of doing it. It never really felt great after that initial glass and then I always just wanted more, which led to great suffering (trying to fill the hole). This anguish continued during an amazing trip I took with my husband and son. I received a direct experience of "Wherever you go there you are."

We all have ideas of happiness. Europe has always been at the top of my list. I traveled there with my mom when I graduated college and again with my ex-husband several years later. I had not been with my current husband (of 16 years) and our son, and It was something I always wanted to share with them. Finally, we had the trip of a lifetime planned. We were supposed to travel Europe for a year, spending several months in our selected countries. My husband and I were both working on creative projects and we were also homeschooling our son. Europe seemed like the perfect place to be inspired and share an incredible experience. We started our journey in Portugal and while it was amazing in so many ways, I knew it was going to be a bit difficult for me. First of all, Portugal has the most amazing wine. The varieties are delicious, super strong and insanely cheap. A wine drinkers paradise. Great tasting wine for $4.00. At the time I wasn't viewing wine as something toxic, instead it was my lifeline. I was still under the illusion that wine was something I needed in order to be happy. Once we landed in Europe, my addiction faced me head on. If I'm being honest, it actually faced me on the flight over there. Our flight included wine with our meals and everyone else was drinking copious amounts, so why not?

I already knew Europe was alcohol central. Day drinking is almost expected. In Portugal they even have these little shops where you go get a shot of Ginja, a Portuguese liquor made from cherries. It is considered perfectly normal to stop by a Ginja shop in the morning or any other time and pay a dollar or two for a quick shot before you go sightseeing. Talk about a bad habit. I liked the taste of Ginja and the buzz it gave me. I found it a bit unsettling that there were shops on every corner like Starbucks. I definitely didn't need to start taking Ginja shots every few hours. I was already tempted to drink more than I did in the states as Europe is filled with romantic cafes, beautiful restaurants, drinking spots by the sea, perfect settings to "tie one on" whenever the mood strikes you.

In the states I never allowed myself to be a daily "wine with lunch "drinker, but while in Europe it seemed normal. Maybe if you are on a two week vacation you can justify partaking in this, but we were supposed to be living in Europe for a year. I knew this was not a path I needed to go down. I was already psychologically addicted to alcohol. I was painfully aware of the fact that I would return to America with a full-blown drinking problem if I started day drinking on a regular basis. That's the moment I really started to face myself. I was in Europe with my family on an adventure of a lifetime and I was bummed out because it couldn't be a drunk fest. I wanted to plop down in every cafe and drink the day away while people watching and perusing museums. Isn't this what you are supposed to do in Europe? I couldn't imagine being there and not at least having a good buzz on most of the time. I started to use all my "rules". I would share a carafe of wine at lunch with my husband. I had gotten him on board with drinking in Europe (at least initially), then I would have a spritz or two in the evenings or maybe more wine. I wouldn't allow myself any more than that. So pretty much I was starting to drink a bottle of wine per day (something I didn't do in the states). I realized after about a month of this, I felt like crap. That's when the phrase hit me "Wherever you go, there you are." Even in Europe I was addicted. My mental obsession with alcohol was ruining my experience.

When we got to France, I changed my rules to only the carafe with lunch and then one glass of wine with dinner. Then when we got to Italy, I dropped the day drinking and would just have one or two glasses with dinner. By the end of the trip I was barely even drinking because it wasn't fun to face the reality that I just always wanted more. There was always another cafe, another carafe of wine. My love affair with alcohol really did end in Europe, I just didn't realize it until a few months later. I was becoming aware of the fact that whatever I was needing was not helped by more alcohol. I was getting a glimpse into the realization that drinking wasn't a path to happiness, in fact, it was the complete opposite. It was a path to misery and shame. I could no longer run away from my psychological addiction to alcohol. Even in the midst of the most wonderful family adventure, it was at the forefront of my mind. Looking back I understand this was a blessing as I was starting to recognize the control alcohol had over me. I wanted my power back, and I was finally noticing all the ways my addiction was stealing it. My mind was starting to compare this situation to a bad relationship. The honeymoon phase of alcohol had probably ended for me about 25 years ago, but I continued to be involved and couldn't let go. When comparing it to a destructive and toxic physical relationship, I guess you could say I hadn't been punched in the face yet, but I had definitely gotten some bruises and abuse year after year. Over and over and over again. I wanted to break up with alcohol but was scared of what my life would look like without it. It had always been my crutch (or so I thought). I now realize it wasn't a support but a huge obstacle to any greatness I could achieve. I needed to let go of this toxic relationship. Just like knowing you need to leave an abusive physical relationship even if you don't feel ready. I wanted to leave the wine and be done with it, but I was really scared.

I wish I had known then what I know now. Breaking up with alcohol was not a horrible experience. In fact, it was quite the opposite. When I finally quit for good, I got my life back. I am writing this book, so you will have someone tell you what no one told me. Everything you want is on the other side of your addiction. The alcohol will never make you happy no matter how many times you give it a try. Nothing will change until you make the choice to walk away and let it go.

8

MAKING THE DECISION

When we returned from Europe I went back to all of my "rules." I tried to only drink on the weekends. I had a very hard time adjusting to this after drinking daily while abroad, but I was determined not to continue down that path. The problem was, we were living on an island and the beach was a trigger for me. I associated the beach life with drinking. Many days I ended up breaking my rules. During this same period of time, I started really paying attention to my moods. I realized during the week when I was sober, I would feel pretty clear and happy. I would then drink on Friday, Saturday, and Sunday, wake up on Monday and find myself depressed. I had started my meditation practice again and since I was meditating regularly, I was more in tune with my mind and general feeling tone. Once I wasn't drinking multiple days in a row, it was easy to see I was just happier without it. So why did I continue to do it? I think primarily it was out of habit. For my entire adult life I was a weekend drinker, it's just what I did. It's what my parents did and most all my friends. The fact that my husband wasn't into it didn't matter. I jokingly called him "Mr. Serious," "Mr. Uptight," and Teetotaler". I also told him he wasn't raised southern like me and didn't know how to have fun. The truth is, when I really started to examine my mind and feelings, drinking didn't seem all that great. Certainly, I had a list of things that weren't cool about it. I was finding it harder and harder to justify my desire to drink. I thought maybe I could return to being just a "special occasion drinker" or "every other weekend" drinker, but eventually I realized I was just done. Done with putting so much energy into figuring it all out. I didn't want to think about when and if and with whom I would drink. I wanted the simplicity of just being a non-drinker. I didn't want to "sometimes" drink, "mindfully drink" or make up any other pseudo hip titles in order to continue on with a destructive habit. I wanted to really be finished with it all. Once I made this decision, the energy that was freed up in my system was incredible. I finally felt free. The freedom I had always been looking for in meditation, yoga, and any other spiritual practice I had been participating in was right inside of me all along. I just needed to let go of the one huge attachment I had. My attachment to alcohol. Before I quit for good, I never realized how much this drug that almost everyone accepts as a normal part of existence was the true cause of so much of my turmoil and unhappiness. The fluctuations in my mind that were caused by all of this inner struggle were disruptive to any kind of freedom I was searching for. When I stopped drinking it was like my mind could finally settle into stillness. I personally haven't found the decision to quit drinking to be the sad, dreaded moment that some people who give up drinking seem to feel. For me it felt like FINALLY. Finally, I am free of being a slave to this drug and on the road to a much better place. It took a while for me to see the path. I literally just had to shift my perspective from feeling like I was missing out if I wasn't drinking to a feeling of missing out on a healthier, more fulfilling life if I did drink. This shift in my mind made all the difference.

Several months before I made the decision to break up with alcohol, I became super clear on one thing, drinking just wasn't fun anymore. There was a time when I thought drinking was fun. I'm not even sure when that time was because as I mentioned, I started throwing up the first time I drank. I believe this "drinking is fabulous and romantic" concept was a misperception. Something I was supposed to believe because everyone else seemed to think so. However, somewhere during my "drinking career," things changed. Even if I didn't overdo it, I would wake up feeling terrible. I'd have a foggy brain, nausea, headache, and anxiety. In addition to these horrible physical symptoms that came from poisoning my body. It was the mental torture that I hated. The absolutely horrible guilt. Did my husband and I have a fight last night? Is my son mad at me for drinking again? Did I have another emotional outburst? (a "fun thing" I liked to do when loaded), I never got violent, I would just obsess and obsess over things. It could be anything and I would go on and on arguing about nothing. Eventually, I started to realize, the first 10 minutes of drinking was the only part I enjoyed. The ritual of going to the store to procure the alcohol (that's the best part because it's the anticipation of "fun" something to ignite some life into an otherwise "boring, regular" day).

You would think a whole bottle of wine would have gotten me drunk. I'm only 5ft 4 inches and very petite. The reality was that I had a high tolerance from years of drinking and a bottle just didn't do the trick. This is really what started to make drinking unappealing. I had hit a crossroads where I either switched to the hard stuff to catch a faster buzz or continued on with large amounts of wine. Neither of these choices felt good and I realized I was in the throes of addiction. I had taken 30 day breaks before. Mostly to appease my husband and prove to myself that I could take or leave alcohol. I also took breaks to try and lower my tolerance, but after those breaks, my tolerance level would go right back to where it previously was pretty quickly. This brought me to the full realization that drinking only caused me suffering and I was tired of it. I wanted happiness and I knew I deserved to feel good. There had to be a better way of life. Drinking was blocking me from being the best I could be, and I was over it.

I remember the moment I decided I was finally done with drinking. It was the 10 year anniversary of my mom's death and I was drinking mimosas by the pool while feeling sorry for myself. Because my husband wasn't having any, I was shocked when at around 4pm I was out of champagne. I didn't want to be finished drinking so I asked my husband to run out and get more. He responded, "Seriously, you want another bottle?" That's when it hit me, there was never going to be enough alcohol. I had hit a place with my drinking that there was never enough. Never enough to fill whatever hole was inside me. I realized if I didn't stop, I was consciously choosing to continue suffering… always wanting more. I also realized I would be making the choice to transition from being a "moderate to heavy" drinker to a full-blown abusive drinker. This was a scary thought. I decided I would rather give it up totally than go down that road, because we all know how that ends. The moment I decided I was really finished with drinking was not after a night of imbibing too much. The moment I quit was during a drinking stint when I ran out and wanted more. I then realized alcohol didn't contribute anything positive to my life. Only misery. I hated who I had become when I drank, and I knew I was a better person than the one alcohol had morphed me into. I came to the realization that I actually despised alcohol. Alcohol had even robbed me of what could have been a beautiful childhood. My parents were amazing people, but their lives were also ruled by their addictions. I could no longer continue the destructive pattern. I was really done.

How many times have you quit drinking in your mind? You know, the morning after you had one (or four) too many. Your head throbs and you are so very nauseous. You made terrible decisions the night before and you never want to be near a drink again. For me this number was high. I actually did an estimate and this is what I came up with: I have been drinking approximately 35 years. Most of those years I was hung over at least one weekend morning, sometimes both. Sometimes none, but If I'm honest it was more often than not. Most of the time I wouldn't feel great on weekend mornings due to drinking too much. After calculating how many years I have been a drinker and adding up weekends (probably more as I sometimes drank too much during the week as well). I have probably sworn off alcohol at least 1,500 times! How about you?

Do the math and you will be blown away. This is crazy to think about. If I had been doing anything else in my life that caused me that much agony, would it have taken 1500 times of making the same mistake to quit the habit? This makes no logical sense, but this is how addictive alcohol is. Time isn't always your friend in regard to drinking because you forget. You forget all the torment it has caused you. Somewhere in your gut you remember, but when the visceral feeling is gone and you are left with only a memory of how horrible you felt after a night of drinking (physically and mentally). Somehow, this just isn't enough to make you say-No More!

I am no different from others who drink. Eventually if you continue to drink, you will find yourself in a place where you always want more (maybe you are already there)? Recently I was watching an interview with a famous woman who was a heavy drinker, and it was destroying her life. During the interview, the news anchor said, "and that's when she realized she couldn't be a person who drinks safely." I laughed out loud when I heard this as no one can drink safely. Alcohol is a highly addictive drug. Would you play around with using meth or heroin? Thinking you could be one of the "sometimes, safe users of those drugs?" This is a ridiculous idea that some people can drink socially and never become addicted. People believe it because society tells them this lie over and over. If you drink a glass of wine every day, you will eventually want more. If you drink a bottle of wine every night, you probably already want more. The pacing of how quickly we become addicted is different for everyone but there is no denying its addictive. Why do we all take the chance? I'll tell you why. We roll the dice because our society currently revolves around alcohol and if you don't drink (even just a little) you are labeled either a recovering alcoholic, boring, or weird. You must be weird if you just decide not to drink if you aren't an alcoholic. Even though most who continue on the alcohol path eventually face trouble. This is why the term "alcoholic" can be misleading and actually does a disservice to many people. People continue to tell themselves they can drink because they aren't alcoholics. When in reality if you aren't willing to give up a toxic substance that will lead you to become addicted if you aren't already, aren't you already addicted? Do you consider people who snort "a little bit" of cocaine each day addicts? How about a "little bit" of heroin?" Addict? Alcohol is also a drug, no matter what society tells you.

~

We create labels to give ourselves a sense of order and control. These labels can be very misleading. One of the problems I see with the term "alcoholic" is it really is a matter of someone's opinion of what that is, and if you like to drink, you probably have changed your opinion of that term regularly. We conveniently shift our idea of the term to suit where we are in our own drinking. For instance, maybe in the past you had the opinion that people who drink daily are definitely alcoholics. Then when YOU start wanting to drink daily, you shift your perspective to-"people who drink before 5pm are alcoholics." Or maybe you tell yourself you aren't an alcoholic if you only drink weekends even though you are totally blotto all weekend. Perhaps you determine how addicted someone is according to how much alcohol they consume. Telling yourself people who drink more than two glasses have a problem. Then at some point on this fun drinking journey when you want more than two glasses, you tell yourself people who drink a whole bottle are alcoholics. At some point, you need the bottle, so you change your boundary to two bottles. Then you begin to tell yourself people who drink vodka are alcoholics. There is always someone drinking more than you. You can use this fact to make yourself feel better about your own drinking. None of this matters and it's all a game we play with the labels and the comparisons. The reality is, no one is above this torture because alcohol is a very addictive drug, no matter what society and the alcohol industry tells us. The problem with these labels is that they trick "social drinkers" into thinking they are special and that they will always have control of their drinking.

To test this theory, my husband and I decided to make a list of all of our friends and family. We thought certainly we could come up with many people we knew who could control their drinking. We honestly came up with only a couple of people who drink only a few times a year (and that might not even be true, as we are basing this just from what we have been told.) Who truly knows what goes on behind closed doors?

Everyone else on our list was either a non-drinker or someone who drank every night and/or every weekend. So where are the moderate drinkers? Are they the people who drink two glasses every single night? Or how about the weekend bingers, are they the moderate drinkers? Maybe it's the people who just drink at parties?

The term "alcoholic" gives everyone the illusion that it's safe to drink if you don't fit into that term. But that label really is deceptive as it makes the rest of the world think they have a free pass to drink. Sorry to be the bearer of bad news, but you aren't any different from the rest of us humans. The good news is that because you are human and there is no puppet master ruling over you, you also have the choice to just stop today. Take your power back. Quit giving alcohol attention and energy.

I wrote this book after I quit drinking as a therapeutic process and hopefully as something that can be helpful to others. I don't plan to go on blogs or attend meetings with people and continue to talk and talk and talk about something I no longer want in my life. To me that is like breaking up with a boyfriend and then continuing to talk about him every chance I get. How do you ever truly move on if you obsess about something constantly? Knowing my personality and how I am naturally obsessive. I would rather focus on many other things rather than the thing I no longer want in my life. It just doesn't make sense to me. If meetings and blogs are helping you or helped you in the past, that is awesome, keep it up. However, there are people who don't find talking about alcohol helpful. They want to move on.

I have used the techniques outlined in this book which include letting go of the need to think or talk about alcohol very often. I have found great personal success with this method. Shifting your paradigm around alcohol changes everything in a natural, organic way.

9

SHIFTING YOUR PARADIGM

I believe my own paradigm started to shift thanks to my friends. I should call them my angels, because they are. Unbeknownst to them, they each gave me a new message about alcohol. Maybe because I was ready and listening, maybe because I was so tired of my inner turmoil concerning my drinking habits, or perhaps it was just divine grace. I'm not sure how it all lined up, but within a 3 month period, I happened upon three different friends who told me they had quit drinking alcohol.

The first friend was a new one that I met in while our family was traveling and living in Europe. We were staying in Lagos, Portugal and my new friend was also American and living with her husband and son on a huge yacht. We were fast friends as we had many things in common. I was quite sure she most likely loved wine as much as I did, and I was looking forward to spending Christmas on their boat. Well, it turns out this woman and her husband had quit drinking and been sober for several years. I was curious about it, so I asked her why and how she quit. She said, "I woke up one day and was just done." That's all she said. So matter of fact, so simple. She didn't elaborate or anything. I couldn't get her phrase out of my head. I also felt done but didn't quite know how to quit. We continued to have Christmas on their boat and all of the guests drank wine, but my friend and her husband didn't. They still had fun, still were funny, didn't seem like teetotalers, or weird, or boring. They weren't serving us strange mock-tails or pushing their agenda on us. They just did their thing. Still enjoying life. Still enjoying Europe. Just present, sober, and free. I wanted what they had. I wanted to be sober and not need to drink wine to feel like I was having fun on a boat. I wanted to be free of the need I had to drink in order to relax with friends. After enjoying Christmas with my friend, her phrase kept looping in my head. It haunted me actually. I thought of it all the time. The phrase she said to me - "I woke up and I was just done." I also really wanted to be done.

A few months later a similar incident happened. This time with one of my longtime, closest friends. I had just moved to the beach and had opened a bottle of Pinot Grigio and sat down to call her, knowing she would be drinking her Pinot and we could chat all about the new beach house I was living in. When we started talking, she told me she had quit drinking and didn't even miss it. She said it as simple as that, just so easy breezy. Didn't. Even. Miss. It.- I couldn't imagine! I was floored. This woman was like 65 years old and had been drinking white wine her entire adult life. I assumed it was her lifeline, just like breathing. I always thought she loved it even more than I did. How could she just quit? Just like my other friend, she just up and decided. I didn't ask her to elaborate even though I was happy for her. I was shocked and felt guilty asking for more details while I continued to drink my pinot. However, her words stuck with me. "Didn't even miss it." This phrase also started to loop in my head.

Then there was my third friend. This was a friend I hadn't seen in 20+ years. We met for lunch about two months before I quit drinking. She had been a huge boozer back in the day and when we met for lunch, I assumed we would be kicking back with some wine. I was wrong. The minute we sat down to eat, she informed me she had recently quit drinking. She told me she had been sober for about 4 months. "I haven't felt this good in years," she told me. I asked if she went to AA.

She said, "No, I don't want to go and listen to people talk about alcohol." Right then it struck me. Three friends in the past three months told me they had quit drinking. No AA, no rehab, nothing. I looked at it as a message from the universe. At the time, even though I was so happy for this friend and her sobriety, I was actually quite disappointed we couldn't reminisce about the past 20 years over wine. We actually ended up having a great visit anyway (imagine that). Her words stuck with me and she looked amazing. I told her I still loved wine and she said she had too until it had taken her dignity away. She went on to tell me a very sad story of how she fell to the ground while in a ball gown in front of her neighbor. I listened with intrigue as I also felt I had lost my dignity in about a million different ways over the years. Suddenly it occurred to me that we all have different reasons for finally saying goodbye to alcohol. I realized I didn't need to wait for the label of "alcoholic" to quit. I started to understand the idea that I could quit drinking even if I didn't think I was an alcoholic.

Each of these friends offered me such a gift with their words. These women made me realize the decision to quit drinking didn't have to be some huge, dramatic thing. I could just do what they had done. Just say it and make it so. This was a major realization for me. I had somehow forgotten that I am in charge of my life and when something is causing me so much turmoil, I have the power to "just say no", as they used to say in the eighties. Turns out that phrase isn't just helpful for kids. Grownups can walk away from peer pressure too. I had always assumed when I decided to stop drinking (which I had been considering for a long time), that it would turn into a huge ordeal and I might even have to go to therapy or a group or something. The idea of it being simple had truly never occurred to me. Their words kept going through my head the next month. "I don't even miss it," "I just woke up one day and was done," "I feel amazing. I haven't felt this good in years." These words became the new recording in my mind. I couldn't quit thinking that if these women who I loved and admired and felt camaraderie with could quit so easily, I could too. So, one day, a few months later, I found my own phrase - "This isn't fun anymore"- and that was that.

I don't mean to trivialize the decision to stop drinking. Especially if you have a chemical dependency, it won't be easy, and you will need support. However, if you are a "moderate to heavy" social drinker, you are most likely only psychologically addicted. This means when you learn to change your thoughts, things will be easier. When you stop drinking, initially your mind will play all kinds of tricks on you. When I first stopped, after about a week or so, my mind would start envisioning situations where I would most likely be tempted to drink. Even though my paradigm had shifted in regard to drinking and I viewed it as something I no longer needed. My subconscious mind still had the pattern of being attached to alcohol. I would start thinking about a friend's wedding or some other situation where I might want some champagne or wine. Even though I was literally having zero cravings for alcohol in the present moment. When these thoughts would arise, I would tell myself, "Yes but if you had that one taste you know it would taste terrible as you aren't used to that toxin anymore and then you would probably drink it anyway and then the pattern would start all over again. Is that worth it?" My answer was ALWAYS no and then I would quickly shift my train of thought to the present moment or a positive memory or idea.

I am certain that this process helped me immensely as my mind was continuing to learn to view alcohol as an unhealthy substance that I didn't want or need. You see we have to retrain our brain. Whether you have been drinking for 20 or 30+ years or even 5 or 10. Your brain pattern is one that desires alcohol and views it as positive. Even if you are to the point where you see all the negative repercussions that come from consuming it. You have a pattern. Just like brushing your teeth or an exercise routine. If you have always had a drink every night or every weekend or every celebration. Your mind just goes into autopilot. You really are rewiring yourself to think differently and no one can do this for you. That's one reason I titled this book "No Thanks, I Don't Drink. My New Mantra" as it seriously is a mantra of mine now and it can be yours too. This way your mind starts to believe you are a non-drinker, because you now are! Your mind can either be your enemy or your ally in life. The choice is yours.

10

LIES + ENTERTAINMENT

Once you stop drinking, you will realize you have been duped. You will finally see alcohol for what it is: a glamorized and toxic substance. You will also start to notice how many people drink.

Why isn't sober considered the norm? Most people acknowledge that meth heads and crack users are hurting themselves and need to "clean up their act." Why is alcohol so widely accepted and not treated as if it is a destructive drug? This is one reason it seems so hard for people to quit. The group mindset is this - If you don't drink you are missing out and life is boring. From a young age we are programmed to believe that regular consumption of alcohol is natural, and a much needed substance to have in our lives. Other drugs are considered bad and dangerous. This is not the case with alcohol. If you don't drink alcohol, people assume you are an alcoholic, a super conservative religious person, or just a bore. This is completely ridiculous. We need a new narrative. A true picture of what a life ruled by alcohol really looks like.

My reality has proven otherwise. I have found the sober life to be fabulous! My mind is more focused, my body more toned, my relationships are healthier, my sleep is better, my overall mood is better, my eyes are brighter, my mindset is more positive, etc…So why all the lies about how great drinking is? Because keeping us hooked means big money to the alcohol industry. They want us addicted. In order to quit you must shift your perspective. Be grateful you have been given a gift to realize how terrible drinking is for you. Know that your life will become infinitely better when you choose to quit. Shifting your mindset is much easier when you have a regular meditation practice (I will discuss this later in the book.) Meditation will help you operate from your internal self instead of being guided by the external world.

Each moment becomes a bit more sweet when you are living a sober life. Mostly because you don't have a poison coursing through your veins that adds negativity and pain to your existence. When I was a drinker, I felt like I was in a permanent kind of arm twisting with myself. Once I decided to let go of alcohol and its grips on me, it was like my entire system just went "Ahhhh" and let go. I was released from of all the negative ways alcohol was impacting my life. Not just externally but also internally. My entire body, mind, and especially my spirit. I could relax into who I really was without expending so much energy on trying to decide whether or not I should continue drinking. When I finally quit for good, the reason I no longer felt like I was missing out on something (like all the times before when I would "take breaks from drinking,") is that I shifted my perspective about alcohol. You won't have success in quitting, if you don't do the same. You will always feel like everyone else is getting to have fun while you are over in the corner sulking and not drinking. When you shift your paradigm, you will realize this is just not true. Society and the alcohol industry have brainwashed us.

Is it fun to most likely destroy every meaningful relationship in your life because alcohol is your one true love? Is it fun to damage your brain each time you drink? Is it fun to realize your focus is warped and you now have terrible memory recall? Is it fun to make bad decisions and have huge regrets after a night of drinking? Is it fun to carry around guilt and shame all the time? Think of all the negative ways alcohol affects your life. Then imagine yourself giving it up and picture how you would feel.

The main reason it is hard to picture yourself thrilled to give it up is because of what you have been programmed to believe. If you examine what it really going on, reality tells a completely different story. Start telling yourself the true story and your mind will start shifting its views. When I see people at the grocery store with their carts full of wine and beer, I don't envy them. I want to help them. I know that many people are just like I was. Tired of the hold that alcohol has on them but not feeling like they are addicted enough to need AA. This is the reason that while I think AA is great for the people it helps, there are many of us who fall in the middle. We are social drinkers who really want to stop before becoming chemically addicted. By the way, that means everyone, because anyone who drinks socially will continue to become more addicted. It might take twenty years instead of five or ten, but no one gets a free pass with drugs. The smart thing to do is quit today before your life is completely out of control. Don't put it off and continue to have the stupid rules about when and where you will drink. Just do it for real this time. Shift your mindset and everything will change. When you start to look at your reality with new eyes, you will notice how much alcohol is glamorized in the media. Magazines, television shows, and movies are where most of the drinking is happening.

I remember a friend saying to me, "Ashlee, your husband doesn't know how much most women drink. I wouldn't even consider your weekend wine a problem. Look at the reality shows, those women drink vodka in the morning." Her comment validated what I thought. These shows and movies make people feel better about their own alcohol consumption. Just like they make themselves feel better by comparing themselves to friends and relatives who may drink more than they do. Now they can also compare themselves to television shows and movies where the actors drink at all hours and still look and feel fabulous.

First of all, the middle-aged women drinking large amounts of alcohol would not look thin nor feel fabulous. If they were drinking as much as they imbibe on these shows, they would be overweight, loose skinned, anxious, and depressed zombies. They wouldn't feel like dressing to the nines each day and the show would mostly consist of them hinged over the toilet early in the morning and then on the couch the rest of the morning nursing a terrible hangover. The way the people on the shows drink, the hangover would most likely last all day. Instead of great outfits, they would be in sweats with muffin top bellies. Yet somehow these women who eat popcorn for dinner and drink bottles of wine at night, look like they just stepped off the runway. In reality, these women would probably start getting the munchies once they drank the bottle and continue to eat whatever was in their fridge and then maybe even throw it all up. They would gain 15 lbs in two weeks and feel like crap most days. But this isn't what we are shown. We have become zombies to the brainwashing of the entertainment industry and everyone else who wants to sell us on the fact that we can overindulge in toxins and still look and feel fabulous. Maybe you can get by with some of this in your twenties but thirty isn't far behind and reality will start to show itself. We really are what we eat and drink. Beauty comes from the inside out. Not just how you look but your demeanor and soul are affected as well. Like my mother used to say, "Pretty is as pretty does." Drinking all the time just isn't pretty no matter what the latest television series tells us.

When it comes to real life and how moms are portrayed, the "moms who drink are cool" culture is actually quite ridiculous. Let me ask you this- if your mom drank all the time when you were growing up, did you think it was cool? I sure didn't. I remember being terrified my mom was going to die. Watching her get completely bombed out of her mind and oblivious to the world. I would just wonder - "Why does she hate her life so much?" Living in a world with parents who drink all the time is a confusing place for a child.

I find it interesting that as women we have come so far regarding our rights, power, etc... and yet television and movies continue to portray strong women as total lushes? True power does not come from a bottle of wine. Why are we sending this message? Why do we buy into it? Are these the role models we want for our kids? Teaching our children that true happiness comes from a bottle? If you picked up this book, you are most likely wanting to quit drinking as you realize it in no way makes you happy.

One evening my son and I were watching a film together and literally every single scene had people drinking. Even my son said, "Talk about promoting alcohol." The film featured a gorgeous and happy couple. They were on a boat drinking, in a restaurant drinking, at home drinking, at laser tag drinking, in the tub drinking, in the car drinking. It was absurd. The message was this - there is no way these people can have a good time without drinking. I was left thinking, "It will be amazing if my son grows up without ever taking a sip of alcohol when everything he watches, reads or listens to gives him the impression that he needs alcohol in order to live a happy life."

I remember my best friend told me her grandfather promised her brother he would buy him the car of his choice if he could graduate from college without ever drinking. I knew when she told me this that he would fail the challenge. How could he not with the constant pressure? The reality is the pressure doesn't stop when we are kids. We have relentless peer pressure to drink even as adults and I'm convinced this is the #1 reason many people find it hard to stay sober. The trick is to QUIT LISTENING TO SOCIETY. Listen to your inner voice that tells you it doesn't feel good to have the guilt and shame. Listen to your inner voice that tells you life will feel better without alcohol. Listen to your inner voice that tells you that you are strong enough to do this. You deserve better. You deserve a full life that feels good without the repercussions of a night of drinking.

How confusing for all of us, including our children. We have been fooled. Alcohol is a depressant. Do you ever wonder why almost everyone you know is on an antidepressant? Could it have something to do with the FACT that alcohol is a depressant and all those same people drink? I am certain this is no coincidence (it certainly wasn't in my case). This means massive amounts of money for Big Pharma and Big Alcohol. They get you hooked, and the cycle continues. More suffering means more people trying to stop the pain with more alcohol and more pills. This never-ending cycle just continues to pay Big Pharma and Big Alcohol.

I personally grew tired of being a mouse in their drug trap.

11

PEOPLE SAY IT'S A DISEASE

As I mentioned earlier, when I stopped drinking, I didn't go to rehab or any kind of support group. Mostly my husband was my support. Granted I wasn't physically addicted to alcohol, I was mostly a weekend drinker. I noticed how much alcohol was affecting my life in a very negative way and I decided to stop. I was at a very important juncture in my life. I knew if I continued down the path I was on, I would eventually become physically addicted to alcohol.

This makes me wonder, is alcoholism really a disease or is it just something that can happen to absolutely anyone if they keep at it long enough? Alcohol is an extremely addictive drug (no matter what the alcohol industry tells us). Isn't everyone susceptible to this or is it just hard-core drugs like meth and coke that we can all become addicted to? I know several people who have quit cannabis, cocaine, meth, heroin, pills, etc... yet they keep on drinking, telling themselves alcohol is harmless. Do you really believe a person can start with one glass of wine per night and never have the urge to want more? From what I have observed, (in regard to myself and my friends), is that we all started with one glass per night, then we wanted two, then the bottle, and so on. Maybe we are all different in how quickly we shift from wanting/needing just a glass to then drinking the whole bottle, but we all become addicted in some form.

Why mess around with a substance that will eventually make you a slave? I don't know anyone who is immune to this.

If you are reading this and starting to arrive at your own "crossroads" concerning alcohol, stop today. Don't go another day or week wondering when you should do it. Get your life back. You will be so happy you did.

From the first night that you decide to stop you will start to get your self-esteem back. Do you even realize how low it's been? I didn't for the longest time. A few months before I quit, I had started telling my husband (when I was drinking of course) that I had never had such low self-esteem. I blamed him and our marriage. I told him I was unhappy with everything in my life. I didn't realize it was because of my own inner turmoil. I hated that I drank, and this was causing my feelings of self-loathing. Once I made the decision to stop, it was like I got my soul back. I no longer avoided looking in the mirror in the morning because I didn't want to see my bloated face with the dark circles. I didn't need to avoid myself anymore. I remember after a couple of months without wine, I noticed my eyes had this amazing whiteness to them. The toxins were gone, and I could see my real eyes. It didn't take long for me to find self-love again. I wish I had made this decision much earlier in life.

Sadly, most people who need to quit drinking today before it destroys their lives are constantly looking for reasons to justify why they aren't an alcoholic. Everyone wants permission to drink. They want someone to say. "Go ahead and drink every single day. You are special and will always have control and never become addicted." Quit worrying about the labels and realize it's not the smart choice. Unless you are a person who really doesn't drink except maybe a couple of times per year, you are playing with fire. Choose a better game to play.

PART TWO

THE PATH TO HEALING

This section of the book includes all of the practices I utilized to stop drinking. I was already doing most of these things even before I broke up with alcohol, but somehow everything deepened and became more authentic once I cut out all alcohol and drugs. I no longer had the tortured feeling of living a life that didn't resonate with my true nature.

An important step on the path to sobriety is to get real with yourself about your own patterns around alcohol and other drugs. After you have done this and are clear about your history and tendencies, you can proceed with implementing the practices in the following chapters. You might already use some of the techniques I discuss. That is fantastic! You may find that your passion and commitment to these activities will deepen once you quit drinking.

There is no chronological order regarding how you should use these activities. They are lifestyle practices that you will include in your day on a regular basis. The premise of this book is that you aren't missing anything positive when you stop drinking alcohol. The key to understanding and really believing this is to create a life that doesn't include alcohol. When you start to focus on all of these new and wonderful habits, your desire for alcohol will naturally fall away. You can view these techniques as a way to fully commit yourself to a yogic lifestyle. Or, if you aren't a yogi, you may choose to see these methods as tools to a more vibrant life.

12

POSITIVE THOUGHTS = POSITIVE LIFE

Maybe you are tired of the way alcohol is having a negative impact on your life and you are thinking of stopping. If so, this is great as you have already started telling your mind you don't really like this substance. Until you want to not drink, you will drink. It really is that simple. Most people turn quitting into a huge ordeal, but the mind is a powerful ally if you allow it to be. The process of giving up alcohol can be as simple or as difficult as you make it. If you are trying to stop because someone else thinks you should or even because this book tells you to, you won't quit. You will stop drinking when your own mind decides not to drink anymore.

We all have a different path of arriving at that place. The key to stopping is getting your mind there first. This is especially true if you don't have a chemical dependency. If you aren't clinically addicted to alcohol (yet), then the majority of your "addiction" is in your mind. You can either use your mind as a powerful tool or be ruled by it and live your life like a leaf being blown in the wind. Having no control and swaying this way and that. You and only YOU can make the decision to use the power of your mind to create the life you want.

Start visualizing yourself doing other things. You would be amazed how much you actually think about alcohol. When to pick it up, what store, what will you drink, who will you drink with, what party, what time, what event, how much you will you drink, dreading the hangover, etc… Begin to get excited about other hobbies. There is so much energy that is freed up once you fully commit to not drinking. When you continue to have "one foot in one foot out" your thoughts are still thinking of it. As long as you are thinking of it, it has power. You can also train your mind to think negatively about alcohol as I did. I found this so helpful initially, even before I stopped completely. I would think of all the things I didn't like about the way drinking affected my life. I would tell myself I wanted to be healthier and not dependent on something (even if just emotionally) and then eventually, once I stopped drinking, I just quit thinking about it and its power over me was gone. I finally felt free. This is one way having a meditation practice is invaluable when it comes to mind power and focus.

The decision to quit drinking has most likely been building within you for quite some time. That is great! That means you have already been going over in your head the things you don't like about being a drinker. The hangovers, the weight gain, the damage to your organs and skin, guilt, remorse, foggy brain, relationship struggles and on and on. Having already thought of these things, you are mentally making your list of all the ways alcohol is negatively impacting your life. Take a moment or so and write down your own list. I know my list is much longer than what I wrote on this page. It is important for you to start the process of telling yourself how much you dislike what this toxic drug is doing to you. We have been so programmed by everyone to believe this drug is ok and fun but if you really do a legitimate check in, you will start seeing the truth. This is the first step.

Even if the world doesn't change its perspective regarding alcohol consumption, if you are wanting to quit, the key to success is changing your own perspective. Instead of having the idea in your mind that you are supposed to drink, try telling yourself that alcohol is a damaging poison (which it is) and that you don't want to ever put things like that in your body. You want a body that is pure, fresh and alive. Poisoning your cells with alcohol only leads to disease (dis-EASE) and sadness. You want a mind that can focus and remember things. Why would you ever want even a drop of something so bad for you? If you can retrain your brain to think this way, saying no to drinking will be much easier. People make it hard on themselves when they are constantly just thinking of all the fun they are missing out on. However, if you truly examine things, where is the fun? Fun is having a body and mind that feel amazing every day. Being able to hop out of bed feeling fabulous and ready for the day ahead of you. Having cells and organs that are thriving and healthy, not inflamed and deteriorating. Telling yourself this daily retrains your brain to think of alcohol as the toxin that it is.

Once I discovered all the negative ways alcohol was affecting my life. I was clear I wanted to be rid of it. I then began the practice of appreciation. I know it sounds cheesy, but it works! I have personally found thinking better thoughts to be extremely helpful. We are so programmed to think and lean towards the negative. My mother taught me this skill. She constantly complained about what was wrong in her life, our lives, everyone's lives. I was her sounding board, and she would ramble on about her troubles. She was not unusual. Most people live this way. When you grow up with this as your "normal" it can be very hard to reshape the patterns of thought in your own mind. As a child I was highly empathic and would often retreat to my bedroom to look out my window and imagine I was a princess in a faraway place. I wanted to escape my present circumstance and imagination was my only way out. Even as a young girl, I used my mind to escape to a positive place. I somehow forgot this wonderful technique of daydreaming. As I got older, I stepped right into patterns of fear, worry, and negativity. My yoga practice would help for a few hours. I would experience some bliss and gratitude, and then later in the day, come down to reality and start moaning about life. I read uplifting books, definitely used marijuana and alcohol to escape the turnings of my mind but none of those methods would have a lasting effect. Alcohol and pot actually gave me more vrittis (Sanskrit for mind turnings). What has worked in keeping my mind calm and less reactive is having a consistent meditation practice, making gratitude lists, and listening to positive uplifting talks and classical music.

I had to completely retrain my mind to think better thoughts. Not just "positivity", but truly looking for the good in all situations. This is no easy feat and has been a huge challenge, but the rewards have been immense. I have noticed not only my internal environment improving but also my external.

Currently I live in a house one block from a beautiful ocean with a private beach, I have banana and avocado trees in my backyard and a pool in my front yard. A year ago, I only dreamt of a house like this and now it's a reality. Before moving into this house, my husband, son and I traveled around Europe. Even writing that sentence feels like a dream. This is a dream that I turned into a reality. I have found it incredibly fun to realize I have this power! The cool thing is, we all have the ability to turn our thoughts to form. So be careful what you think. Keep your thoughts positive and your vibration high. I had to learn this the hard way. It was in front of me all along, but sadly alcohol and drugs were blurring the path. As your thoughts change, your world changes. Once you do the mental work and your thoughts start shifting, alcohol will no longer be as tempting or attractive as it once was. Your desire for addictive substances will begin to dissipate.

13

FINDING YOUR WHY

A good question to ask yourself is- "Why do I want to get sober? "If you have ever participated in sales you have probably heard the phrase - "Finding Your Why."
Here's a back story about what a "why" is- I launched my own skincare business when I felt I wanted to contribute more to our family finances and yoga teaching wasn't cutting it. I started teaching yoga because I loved it and wanted to share it with people. Making money from it was a bonus and when I was in my twenties, I made enough to survive. I also had some inheritance money and honestly that is mostly how I existed on a yoga teacher's salary. Once we had a child, I needed to make more money and I didn't want to turn my yoga teaching into a business. I decided if I was going to sell something, I didn't want it to be yoga. So I got into skincare sales. One of the first things they teach you in sales is to find your why. This means, why are you doing this? For me, I wanted more money for my family. Salespeople have figured out that it isn't always an easy business, so the key to your success and staying motivated is to remember why you got started. This way when the going gets tough and you run into obstacles, you will keep going. This same technique works in regard to abstaining from alcohol. When the obstacles and urges come, you have something to fall back on. Your "why."

I have a friend who has been sober for about 20 years now. She and I were drinking and pot smoking buddies back in the day. I asked her a few years ago why she quit drinking and she said (in a very matter of fact way) "I can't drink because then I go and sleep with strangers." She was razor clear on her why and I could tell nothing would stand in her way of staying sober. She had a great deal of clarity about why she didn't drink. I was positive this was why she had never gone back to it. We all have our "why" of why we want to stay sober. This why needs to be at the forefront of our minds. It is part of the mind retraining. Instead of thinking of why you want to drink, start thinking of all the reasons you don't want to drink. You most likely have several, but there is probably one main reason you can pinpoint and focus on. In fact, you will probably be hard pressed to find any benefits or really good reasons to keep drinking if you are honest with yourself.

To find your why, think about the one thing you can't stand that you do when you drink (there might be several) but there is a reason you picked up this book, so there is probably a major reason you want to stop. Some people sleep with random strangers when they drink, some people drive while drunk, some people take off their clothes in public or say things they really regret, some have affairs (emotional and/or physical), some start physical altercations, some rage at their children, etc…

For me it was starting arguments with my spouse. I never got violent or raged, but oftentimes when I drank, I would pick ridiculous fights with my husband. He has a temper of his own, so not to say he was always Mr. innocent, but most of the "drinking" arguments were started by me. I might not do it every time I was drinking, but on certain occasions "dark Ashlee", as he liked to call me, would rear her head. We would be having a perfectly wonderful evening and then something would trigger me, and I would just get frustrated about everything. Until I stopped drinking, I didn't realize exactly how irritated I had become. I still remember the tortured feeling this was, to feel super frustrated and just downright mad at life. This is no way to exist. I don't mind feeling angry or frustrated, but to continue to give myself regular alcohol induced aggravation seemed absurd. The longer I kept drinking, the more intense these feelings got. Mostly I was angry at myself, but this anger presented itself in other ways. Mostly blame. Blaming my husband, my parents, my teachers, the world, or even the dog. I was avoiding facing myself and the fact that drinking was no longer serving me (and really never had).

People in denial about their drinking do this all the time. They make jokes about how much they drink; they find others to drink with who drink more than they do, they leave partners who don't agree with their drinking, lose friends who might confront them about it or don't drink enough. All the while walking around with such a huge amount of self-loathing. Deep down they know they are on self-destruct, but they are so angry at everyone else about it. Because this pattern is so familiar, it is often hard to step away from. Finding your why can be a significant step in the right direction. Why do you want to quit drinking? You can look at the list you made earlier and pick your most important reason.

I have a very long list of reasons why I stopped drinking, but my most important "why" is that I love my family more than alcohol. Should I ever have an urge to drink, all I have to do is remind myself that when I don't drink, my family life is more peaceful. Alcohol fuels anger and I want a tranquil home life for all of us. Alcohol does nothing to foster tranquility and peacefulness. I decided to choose peace for myself and my family instead of alcohol induced chaos.

Once you figure out your own why, it will keep you focused and on the right path and you will lose any desire to turn back to a life of angst, frustration, despair, and regrets.

Along with finding my "why," I started to reevaluate everything I had been told about alcohol. An important step in retraining my brain regarding how it thought about alcohol was to start telling myself the truth. Here are some of the things I started to think about:

I would think about how amazing my mornings would feel when I was free of any kind of hangover.

I would think about how my yoga and meditation practice would benefit from a mind and body that wasn't filled with toxins.

I would think about how happy my son would be that his mom was sober all the time.

I would think about how healthy I would really be and feel if I cut out alcohol totally.

I would think about how I felt more empowered, confident, smart, relaxed, free, and at ease when I didn't drink.

I would think about how clear and focused I would feel without a hangover haze.

I would think about how great my relationships were when I didn't drink.

I would think about how I was no longer killing my brain cells on a regular basis.

Even though I was choosing to focus on positive thoughts. I also found it helpful to remember the negatives of drinking:

I would think about hangovers and how I never wanted to feel them again.

I would think about how I started unnecessary fights with my husband.

I would think about how my child deserved to have a sober mom.

I would think about my yoga teacher in India who told me to stop drinking because it would hinder me on the path of yoga.

I would think about how both of my parents died from cancer and how drinking contributed to their disease. I do not want to die young.

I would think about how much I disliked myself when I drank too much.

I would think about how unfocused, depressed, unhappy, and confused I felt when I was a drinker.

Once I started contemplating these thoughts, the appeal of drinking started to fade. I could no longer blissfully enjoy alcohol as these thoughts were with me all the time. The more negative things came into my mind, the less fun drinking became and then at some point it was literally like I'm either a complete masochist or a total idiot. I realized there was nothing positive about drinking anymore. I honestly started to wonder if there ever was. I thought about the "relaxation" aspect of alcohol and started to question whether drinking really relaxed me. Once I reflected on this, I came to the realization that alcohol didn't give me a sense of calm. Instead, I mostly felt unsatisfied and disgruntled after imbibing. I definitely felt more relaxed and balanced from meditation, without any side effects.

Also, regarding feelings, now that I am sober, I love experiencing all emotions as they make me feel alive! Especially true feelings, not just weird alcohol induced emotions. Who wants to walk around a numbed-out zombie? Feelings are what make us human. We have definitely become a culture that promotes numbing any uncomfortable feelings. This is really quite sad. Feelings encourage us to write novels, create poetry, play music, and paint. What is the point of living a life of numbness? Forget being comfortably numb (even though this is one of my favorite songs). I don't want to numb my life. Now my experiences are raw, vivid and full of color. I took off the drunk goggles and will never wear them again.

Once I started telling myself the truth about alcohol, I shifted into a different paradigm. I got my mind on board before I quit drinking, and therefore, when I stopped it didn't feel like a difficult process. What I felt was relief. I was finally rid of something I no longer wanted in my life.

I used this same trick when I quit smoking cigarettes years ago. I would focus on how disgusting it was and all the things I hated about it. To this day I still don't want a cigarette. The mind is a powerful tool. When you train your brain to be grossed out by something, it is hard to crave it. Many people stop drinking, only to start up again because in their mind, alcohol is still something they idolize. Society continues to tell them alcohol is great. This is part of the brainwashing. To truly not have a psychological addiction to a substance anymore, you have to do your own brainwork regarding it. Otherwise, it will constantly be this willpower, white knuckling struggle.

Have you ever changed your mind about something or someone? Ever liked a person, only to later detest them? By the way, I am not saying you should detest anyone. I just know we are all human and have had these feelings. You can do the same thing with an addiction you are trying to kick. Keep reminding yourself why you don't like the substance anymore. Say things like "oh I cannot stand feeling horrible the next day, it's so not worth it." Or "after the initial buzz alcohol just makes me sick." Or "I hate fighting with my spouse when I drink. I always say and do things I regret." "My relationship with my kids is better when I don't drink." "I love how peaceful my family is when I am alcohol free. Everyone is happier."

Come up with your reasons and start saying these to yourself whenever you think about drinking. You probably already do this as you have most likely thought about the negative impact drinking has on your life. Instead of pushing these thoughts away, put them at the forefront of your mind. This will start to make drinking less appealing to you. If you can get your mind on board, once you make the decision to quit, things will flow much easier.

14

NOT AN OPTION

A majority of this book is about the mind and how you can train it to view alcohol as something negative that you don't need in your life. This in turn teaches you to abstain from drinking and in the process, you are prevented from living a life where you constantly feel like you are missing out on something everyone else is doing. I need to let you in on something though. This process totally works but it isn't always easy. Just like when you start a new exercise routine, it's not always easy to get up every morning and go to the gym, but you remember how good you feel when you do it. Your brain remembers. You are training your mind to like exercise. Saying no to alcohol is the same. You train your brain to say no because you know the "feel good" moments when you drink are only about 5-15 minutes and the rest feels terrible. The trick is to remember this. It is very easy to slip into old patterns of handling stress, trauma, or just plain old Tuesdays. You have to keep your eye on why you are giving it up for good. The mind can play tricks on you, telling you it is silly to quit when you aren't an alcoholic "yet." Telling you it's ok to just have it "sometimes" when deep down you know better, and that one decision just starts the process all over again. Your mind will trick you if you don't train it to think differently.

A big hiccup for me was when I started dreaming about alcohol. I was about a month into my sobriety when every night alcohol would come up in my dreams. I wasn't always drinking in the dreams but I was faced with the choice to drink or not and sometimes I did. I would wake up in tears because I was so firm about my decision during my waking life, I felt like my mind was torturing me. I realized pretty quickly that my brain and psyche weren't really accepting the fact that I had given up something I had been doing for 30+ years. I used these dreams as motivation. The drinking dreams always felt terrible. I knew I would feel even worse in the waking world if I actually did drink. I didn't want to undo all my positive work. Slowly over time, the dreams stopped. My psyche finally got the picture that we were done. This just proves how strong the mind is and this is where meditation is so very helpful.

I have heard there are many people who stop drinking by using the "day by day" method. Realistically it is obviously always a choice to drink or not to drink each and every day. However, I personally found I had to mentally remove the choice in order to finally abstain. Just like I did with cigarettes. Drugs and drinking were no longer options for me. When I decided I was done with drinking, I told myself I was no longer a drinker. As long as it was an option, I knew I would always find an excuse to do it even though it added nothing positive to my life. I knew old habits die hard and although I wasn't physically addicted, psychological addiction is a powerful force and I didn't want to expend all my energy to keep alcohol at bay. I wanted to move on with my life. Not allowing drinking to be an option didn't leave any room for thoughts of "maybe today" or "sometimes" or "if something catastrophic happens." This is part of retraining the brain. If you live the "day by day" approach, then you are still telling your mind alcohol is something you want that you can't have. Instead, take your power back and retrain your mind to not think of it or want it.

Again, I compare it to a breakup. If you breakup with

someone who is bad for you, do you break up forever? Or are you always thinking of them, wondering about the moment you may decide to take them back? If you shifted your perspective enough to see that they are toxic, why would you take them back? Alcohol is no different. You realize it is toxic, it is a negative substance in your life. Why would you ever want to drink again?

Once you make the commitment to stop drinking for good, you will eventually stop thinking of it so often. You probably don't realize how alcohol is robbing you of mental energy. Especially if you think you are drinking too much, the guilt and shameful feelings constantly zap you of precious energy. You won't realize how much energy is being taken from you until you stop for good. Once you do stop, you will start focusing on many other wonderful aspects of your life. As you start to feel better about yourself, you will have even more energy to dedicate to other things. You will most likely discover new hobbies, passions, and just mundane things to be grateful for. One day you will realize you no longer even think about having a drink. The cravings are gone, and the habit has stopped.

I found after about two months, thoughts about drinking took up less and less of my mental energy. In the past I would always quit for about 30 days. I had it marked on my calendar and I was definitely counting down the days until my "cleanse" was over. I felt like I was missing out the entire time, depriving myself of something I thought I really wanted. There is a special power that comes from deciding you aren't going to ever drink again. Because you are telling your brain drinking alcohol is no longer an option, it quickly retrains your mind not to focus on drinking any more as it is something you no longer do. Think about it like a food that you really like that is terrible for you and all of a sudden it isn't grown anymore. There is no way you can have it, so you forget about it. You can use this same technique with drinking. As long as you make it an option, you will most likely always go back to it. My mind let it go quickly once I mentally decided all the reasons I no longer wanted it in my life. You have got to get your mind on board with this or you won't be successful in stopping. I found it so empowering to be in control of my mind instead of letting it control me. We are the creators of our life. I decided the life I wanted didn't include alcohol anymore and it simplified everything. It really all boils down to choice. You have free will. Life doesn't just happen to us. Every choice we make is important and choices like deciding whether to be a non-drinker or a drinker are major decisions that will alter the trajectory of your life. You can change your mind at any time. Until you change it, you will just go on autopilot and do what you have always done. The great news about all of this is the fact that if you are looking at your own life and not happy with where you are, you have the power to change things. Make the decision and so it shall be.

I encourage you to start checking in with yourself while drinking. Notice your mood and feelings before you drink and then notice how you feel a drink or two into the experience. Maybe you are still in a place where alcohol mostly makes you giddy without any anger, depression, guilt, or shame. I guarantee you if you continue drinking things will shift, they always do with alcohol. Perhaps you are already noticing the feelings of anger, guilt, shame, and sadness arising. You can choose to stop now and save yourself a lot of pain and suffering. You are worth it.

I look back and remember those horrible feelings and mind states that I was giving myself (on purpose if I'm being honest) and I compare it to how I feel now. I think of sitting in meditation and how that feels compared to drinking a few glasses of wine. There is no comparison to the joy meditation gives me compared to the sorrow alcohol brought. Drinking just never gives a happy ending. Think about the reality you are creating for yourself. Do you really want a reality where you are drunk and hungover 1/2 or even 1/3 of your life? Or how about just every weekend?

Life is precious and I personally want to be awake for it. Do you want to spend any more time being wasted? Getting wasted truly is wasting time and you don't get that time back. We only get so many moments in this life. These are serious questions to ask yourself. Many people mindlessly consume alcohol because it is what they have always done. Once you wake up to the lies society and the alcohol industry tell us, it is hard to ignore the fact that regularly consuming alcohol is super destructive. The destruction has most likely already started. Maybe it's ruining your relationships, your job, or your self esteem. It's definitely destroying your mind, body, and soul. At what point will you decide you no longer want a life full of devastation?

For me, that moment was when I noticed my relationships were suffering. It wasn't enough that my self-esteem was in the gutter, my body was bloated and sluggish, my mind was dull, and my soul felt ripped in half. My wake-up moment was when I realized I loved the people in my life more than I loved alcohol. I didn't want to cause them unnecessary suffering any longer. I also loved myself enough to realize I was super unhappy from years of imbibing. I had denied this for a very long time because I didn't want to give up drinking. I blamed everything and everyone else for my unhappiness. I blamed my husband, my age, my genetics, my bank account, my parents, my unfulfilled dreams, etc. The list was endless. Once I stopped drinking all the blame ended. The only person to blame was myself. I was the one who continued to drink even when I knew it was destroying everything dear to me. This realization changed everything. I started to work on fulfilling my dreams again. The alcohol was blocking it all. All the breaks I took, the rules I made around drinking, and any other forms of denial I used, never changed anything. I didn't feel happy again until I broke up with alcohol for good. My soul was then freed from the bondage of the drink. I know it sounds crazy, but it is true. Something shifted and I just wasn't the same. You can have that same transformation; you just have to decide you are worth it. We are all worthy of a beautiful life free of addiction. Using drugs and alcohol is always a choice. Make the right one and watch your life unfold in a completely new direction.

15

THE GIFT OF MEDITATION

I have found a new superpower and it's called meditation. Meditation will change your life. There is nothing quite like it to get you started on the path to a happier, healthier existence. You will learn all about yourself: your mind, habitual patterns, and neuroses. With time, you may also discover your unique gifts and how you can use them to serve others. This leads to a contentment that alcohol and partying will never deliver. A mindful life is the complete opposite of a drunk life. Instead of avoiding and numbing feelings, you face them. You get to know your truest self.

My personal path to meditation was pretty inconsistent. For many years, I was an "on again off again" meditator. I always found it easier to have a dedicated yoga asana (postures) practice. Even though I felt amazing after meditating, I was more drawn to asana because I could move my body. I would tell myself that I was practicing meditation in motion (which is true) and after two hours of yoga, I didn't want to spend more time "just sitting." I would already have my yoga buzz and felt that was enough. When life got busy, my mediation practice was the first thing I would drop.

I had received many glimpses of the power of meditation with all the retreats I had attended over the years. For some reason I resisted making it a priority. Just as I knew I wanted to remove alcohol from my life, I also wanted more meditation in my life. The interesting thing is, once I stopped drinking, I started meditating more regularly. I went from random weekly meditations, to sitting three times per day. The results were astounding. A consistent meditation practice was the missing piece I had been searching for. I believe this is because meditation is an instant way to shift your vibration to a positive state.

For me this has been life changing. I have always been a negative/melancholy kind of person. If you know me, you are probably shocked as I am a master at putting on a mask. I put on my happy face all the time. I was taught that manners are everything and making others feel good is more important than making yourself feel good. The message I received was that unless I put others first, I was selfish. My mother used to tell me I was selfish all the time when I wasn't doing what she wanted. I learned early in life that my needs weren't important and that I needed to get myself out of the equation. I only existed to please others. I agree we should be kind and helpful to other people, but the lesson I received was a little warped. How can you truly be of any benefit to others if you can't find your own true happiness first?

When you choose to start a meditation practice, you are letting yourself know that you are important. Without self love, you cannot truly love others. Getting on your cushion each day is a form of self-love. You make it a priority to check in with yourself and listen to Source, God, or whatever you choose to call your higher power. You become quiet and get in the flow. The rest of your day and life will be better for it. Part of that self-love is not judging your meditation as good or bad. You give yourself some kindness and accept everything as it is. For me, choosing to meditate instead of choosing to drink was one way of choosing self-love. I was telling myself that I love myself enough to choose good habits instead of destructive ones. I had tried to have it both ways for most of my life. I attempted to practice self-love by making healthy lifestyle choices like practicing yoga and eating well, only to destroy my efforts with weekend binge drinking. This led to a very tortured, confused state. When I finally made a commitment to a daily mediation practice everything changed. I couldn't kid myself anymore. The toxicity of alcohol was at the forefront of my mind and I couldn't escape it.

A daily sitting practice will truly change your life for the positive. The most important thing is to have a consistent practice. You can start with guided meditations if that feels easier. Even just 15 minutes per day will be beneficial. Allowing your mind to become more focused and getting in touch with yourself is one of the most healing things you can do. You will start to become addicted to the feeling and will miss it if you don't do it. Somehow when you have a meditation practice everything in life just falls into place. You become connected with source and learn to trust yourself and your intuition. Instead of feeling guilty and shameful for drinking, you will feel proud of yourself for doing something positive for you mind and body. This will lead to a strong sense of self, more productivity and just a general state of well-being.

One of the beautiful things about meditation is that you can't really turn it into a competitive sport. It is just you sitting and being with yourself. There is a simplicity in this that will transform your entire life. I personally have a competitive nature and I have found meditation to be so liberating. I don't compete with anyone as it is a completely internal practice. No one is watching or cares about you sitting with your eyes closed. You don't have to look a certain way, so it leads us away from an ingrained need to please others or worry about what the outer world thinks. For many of us, this is the only time in our day when we can just be. This freedom from the outer world is addictive. You will start to love the way you feel after meditating and your system will crave it. Meditation heals your mind, nervous system, and soul. Instead of craving alcohol which is damaging to your body, mind and spirit, you will begin to crave the solitude of meditation.

I also love asana practice and find it healing on so many levels, but it always had a competitive edge that caused me extra suffering. When you practice in a class in front of others, it is human nature to try and "perform" and be "perfect." Asanas are beautiful and people want to watch. This can be a great tool for teaching and a tool I used for many years, but it can also cause some unnecessary suffering when the focus shifts into "doing it better" than others or becomes some kind of circus performance or a method to achieve a perfect "yoga selfie." This is damaging to the art of yoga and causes extreme narcissism which is the antithesis of the true goal of yoga. I still practice asana but only at home where there is no need to perform or show others my accomplishments. My intention with asana practice is primarily to have a comfortable body to sit in meditation. Instead of the 2 ½ -3 hours of asana I used to commit to for decades, I now only spend about 20-30 minutes on asana a few days per week. My main focus is meditation. This has been freeing on so many levels and has led me to a contentment I never achieved with 2-3 hours of yoga asana practiced in a room with others. For a young person who has a lot of extra energy to burn, an intense asana practice can be very helpful, but many of us continue this well into our 40's and 50's. Since asana becomes our primary focus, we never establish a dedicated meditation practice. This can lead to an injured body, a tired spirit, and a taxed nervous system. I encourage you to start a meditation practice today and make it your primary focus on your path to healing and overall wellness. As I have mentioned, the key to having a successful meditation practice is consistency. Mornings are best as it will give a great start to your day and then the day won't get away from you without it happening.

I personally started looking forward to meditating like I used to look forward to drinking. I like to joke that it has become my new drug but really, it's no joke. I have trained my mind to view meditating as more fun than drinking and in fact it's the truth! It is more fun because the benefits are positive, and this makes life more positive. When I was a drinker, I had a hard time finding any true benefits. When you meditate, your vibration is lifted which just helps everything.

Eventually you may work up to sitting two-three times per day. Morning, lunchtime, and evening. Find what works best for you, but keeping the routine is key. I like to view the evening sit as my true "happy hour." There is nothing better than meditating and some light yoga to aid you in getting the most sound, restful night of sleep. You will awaken refreshed and ready to go in the morning, a world away from boozy nights and hungover mornings.

Here is how to begin: Start with 15 minutes, if that is unbearable for you, try 5-10 minutes for a few weeks. Again, the main thing is to make it a routine. Do not blow it off. It will be so tempting as there are always a million things you need to do. You will look for excuses not to sit. Eventually you will crave it though, so keep at it. If you are already a person who makes exercise a priority, you can think of it like working out. It's a workout for your brain. When you are new to it, it can be hard to get going, just like a new workout plan. Then something shifts and meditation becomes a practice you look forward to because it makes you feel so good. Eventually, you won't let anything interfere with your meditation, but initially it might be challenging to get a routine going.

Find a special spot in your home that will be your meditation area. Keep it simple and make it a cozy, appealing space. You can light a candle, burn incense, or perform any other rituals to help make the area feel sacred.

After your morning bathroom and teeth brushing routine you can begin your meditation:

1. Set a timer for your allotted time. I recommend starting with 5 or 10 minutes and getting that consistent before adding time. Initially, consistency is more important than duration. Better to start with 5 minutes and make it part of your routine than to be overzealous and try for 20 minutes and not continue.

2. Either sit on a cushion or a chair. You want to be comfortable. Should you choose to sit on the floor, you can fold some blankets and sit on the edge of those instead of a cushion. Wherever you choose to sit, you want your hips relaxed and your pelvis vertical.

3. Once seated, drop your sitting bones into the earth and sit tall. Relax your shoulders and your jaw. Allow your cheeks and the corners of your eyes to soften. Feel your tongue resting in your mouth. Your eyes are soft and can be closed or slightly open looking out past the tip of your nose. Arms are relaxed and hands can rest on your thighs.

4. Notice your head. Make sure not to jut your chin forward, just keep your head neutral and your ears open.

5. Notice your breath. Begin to internally watch your breath. Feel it flowing in and out. There is no effort, just watching. As your mind wanders, just invite it to return to focus on the breath. You aren't trying to stop your thoughts, you just watch them and as you notice your mind wandering, invite it back to watch the breath.

Eventually, your meditation practice becomes something you just do like brushing your teeth. The tricky part is making it a habit. Don't miss a day. Just do it every single morning. If you must have your coffee before sitting that is ok, it just has to be part of your routine. You can eventually meditate in the evening as well, but I recommend you try and get the morning going first. Routine is key to sticking with it. Make it a priority like you've made drinking a priority. Meditation is your new practice. Your life will completely change if you can commit to this daily. This is your superpower and your new habit to reduce stress and focus your mind.

As much as I love and recommend meditation, I have friends who aren't drawn to it. Perhaps you feel the same way. There are other activities that can give you a meditative flow. Have you always wanted to paint, write, create poetry, make music, garden, exercise more? What hobbies are you guided to do that you would have more time to do? Reflect on this and start getting excited. For you see, stopping drinking isn't some terrible, negative experience but a true gift. A gift that will expand your life in ways you can't even imagine. You just have to wrap your mind around this idea and let it start to percolate. Start envisioning what you want. Start focusing on the positive aspects of letting go of alcohol.

16

NATURE + HOBBIES

Nature is healing. Our minds, bodies and spirits need fresh air and sunshine. I have always been an "outdoorsy" kind of person and my passion for this lifestyle grew even more once I got sober. I guess you could say nature is a kind of drug for me. I can be in a terrible mood and once I get outside and get my blood moving, I always feel better. One of my favorite things to do is to go on backpacking trips with my husband and son. There is nothing like unplugging from the rest of the world for a few days and exploring the mountains and/or sea.

There is a reason certain rehab centers and PTSD treatment centers take patients on long backpack excursions. Being in nature is a natural high and resets the energy system. Spending time in nature is amazing for your nervous system and overall health. Forest bathing is even a thing now. You can create your own kind of forest bath by just walking slowly through a beautiful spot in nature and using all of your senses to take it in. Taking time to listen to the birds, watch the sunlight, and feel the earth underneath you. Oftentimes when we have been using drugs or alcohol as a way to turn off our feelings, it can be super healing to reconnect with ourselves through being in nature.

Maybe you have a garden or have always wanted one. You can even bring more plants indoors creating a kind of healing sanctuary for yourself. Watering and taking care of plants just like you are taking care of yourself.

Hiking, backpacking, mountain biking, and rock climbing are some ideas of activities that take you outside. Even just long walks around your neighborhood. Take time meandering and noticing all the life around you. Breathing in the air and feeling the sunshine on your face.

Maybe your new "happy hour" can actually make you happy. Try taking yourself outdoors and appreciating all that life has to offer instead of trying to find it in the bottle. One thing is certain, you will wake up feeling more content and rested after spending an evening in nature than you will from a night out drinking. Just try it and see.

Along with spending a great deal of time in nature, part of my path to full sobriety included reconnecting with activities I love. I have always been active. As a child I enjoyed ballet, tap, jazz, tennis, horseback riding, ice skating, swimming and gymnastics. I was also always on my bike exploring. As an adult I became a runner and then when I found yoga, it combined everything I loved and kind of took over. Even when I was a boozer, I was still active. Since I mostly just drank on the weekends, I never felt like drinking interfered with my exercise or yoga as I would usually take one day off my yoga practice anyway. What I didn't realize (until I stopped drinking) is that alcohol was negatively impacting my fitness and yoga practice in a major way.

After about 60 days of being booze free my energy levels went through the roof. I had also lost some weight, so my body felt lighter for workouts. I had been swimming a lot prior to stopping drinking and I was still swimming almost daily when I quit. I noticed my breathing ability underwater was completely different once I gave up booze. I could hold my breath for two laps instead of one and I wasn't even tired after swimming for about 30 minutes. I was also biking a lot and wouldn't fatigue nearly as early as when I was a drinker. These changes made it very easy and exciting to get myself moving even more. I had boundless energy and my mood was definitely better, both of these factors got me off the couch and outside which gave me even more energy.

I encourage you to pick an exercise (or two) to focus on when you make the decision to give up alcohol. You will find yourself with some pent-up energy (all that energy that used to be spent on drinking and thinking about drinking). What are some activities you enjoyed as a kid? Did you ride your bike a lot or play tennis? How about swimming? Do you enjoy being in nature? You could start hiking. Were you a runner? Have you always thought of running a marathon? Starting a training program would give you a new goal. How about yoga? Part of retraining your brain is to teach it to focus on other things rather than drinking. You will feel great in the mornings once you aren't hungover anymore. Your body will start to crave movement. If exercise isn't your thing, you could start a garden. This gets you outside and moving. The idea is to have a new passion. Something you get excited about and something that lets you free up that new energy. Let your mind wander a bit, start to imagine the new you- feeling great and having more energy. Let go of the self-sabotage and guilt. Step into this new life and get excited about it!

In addition to moving your body, find a new hobby. Many people who are mentally and/or physically addicted to alcohol turn drinking into hobby. If this is you, you need a new hobby! What are some hobbies you enjoy that you never feel you have enough time to do? When you aren't spending time drinking or thinking about your next drink, you will have new energy for the activities you enjoy. Gardening, reading, painting, writing or learning a new language are some ideas. I have found it really helps to have a new focus. You may already do some of these things and wonder how giving up drinking will change anything. Somehow when you give up alcohol for good, the activities you enjoy become even more special. For me, it was like I had a newfound love of things I was already doing. They somehow became more precious. Life has a new glow about it once the effects of alcohol wear off. This can actually happen pretty quickly. Have you ever noticed how the day after a hangover you feel great compared to how you felt hungover? It's like that but permanent. You will just feel better all around and this brings a new effervescence to everything you do.

The key to not ever wanting to drink again is remembering the dullness you used to feel when you drank regularly. It is somehow easy to forget how you used to feel once you start feeling better. I have found it helpful to keep a journal. I journaled a lot when I quit drinking and I often go back and read my entries from that time period. The entries are a constant reminder of how depressed, anxious, and tortured I felt when I was allowing alcohol to have all the power in my life. My entries after quitting were the complete opposite. I felt proud, less anxious, happy and centered.

I know I have talked at length about this, but I must say it again. Along with writing, my favorite practice (which can also be considered a hobby) is meditation. For me, meditation was the missing link to getting sober. I can't stress this enough. Practicing this daily helps you check in with yourself. You are more aware and present with your feelings and your own energy. You learn to step into your power, and you won't want to drink as drinking alcohol robs you of power and deprives you of the life you deserve. You won't settle for a "less than" life anymore. You will also start to become aware of the fact that what society tells you isn't always true. You learn to listen to your own heart. There is a saying that prayer is talking to God and meditation is listening. As you begin to listen, spirit will reveal many more interesting things than what you found at the bottom of a bottle. Gone are the hangovers, regret, destroyed relationships, and despair. These things will be replaced with a new zest for life and a body and mind that will feel healthy and strong. The choice is yours.

The "sometimes drinker" label just doesn't work if you truly want the life that is waiting for you. If alcohol already has control of the wheel, you have got to take it back and not just some of the time. Instead of feeling like you are missing out on something, you will look back and wish you had chosen this path much sooner. It's all in how you view it. This is how life works. You can either think a positive thought or a negative one. When you understand you have this power, you start to notice all the decisions you have made in the past regarding drinking. You don't have to remain on autopilot. If alcohol is causing bad things to happen in your life. Make a different decision. Start a new hobby.

17

GREENS FOR GOODNESS

Along with hours of mediation, writing, yoga, swimming, hiking, and biking, I also adopted a super healthy diet when I quit drinking. For most of my adult life I have been a pretty "clean eater." I was even vegan for a long time. I amped things up once I let go of alcohol.

Before I quit drinking, I would sometimes not eat dinner on the nights I would drink as I didn't want the calories. I preferred to drink my calories instead of fueling my body with healthy food. This was terrible for my system and also left me feeling horrible the next day. A friend told me that greens can help with cravings, so once I wanted to totally abstain from alcohol, I upped my greens in a significant way. My husband had recently done some film work for a health conglomerate television station and he had watched numerous videos about nutrition. He started telling me all about "superfoods" and macronutrients, healthy mushrooms, teas, etc… I plunged into learning about all this and I realized I wasn't as healthy as I thought I was. Healthy eating became a fun hobby to focus on while I was in the first weeks of abstaining. Along with retraining my brain to see how toxic alcohol is, I also started learning about the most healthy things I could put into my body. I was on a mission to feel amazing. My husband had some health issues, and he was ready to change his diet for the better too. We had a blast finding new recipes and cooking together. I didn't even miss happy hour anymore as our weekends were spent reading about and cooking really healthy, yummy food.

Not only did my energy levels soar, but my eyes were white and bright again. If the eyes really are the windows to the soul, alcohol had caused my soul to become dim and tired. Now my soul was shining. I looked and felt about ten years younger. I also lost a huge amount of emotional baggage that my drinking was causing. I didn't realize how much guilt and shame I was carrying around regarding drinking. I loved the feeling of waking up in the middle of the night and not having horrible pangs of guilt about drinking one too many. Not having to wonder if I would feel like crap the next day. It was so liberating to know I would wake up feeling amazing and ready for the day. Once you start feeling so good, you won't want the feeling of a hangover ever again. You will realize it is just not worth it. Why sacrifice feeling amazing for something so temporary? You will stop wanting to ingest such an unhealthy substance into your body. Alcohol will lose its appeal once you reap the benefits of abstaining.

I have included some recipes in this book as healthy eating is key to helping you feeling good while you detox. Even if you already eat healthy foods, if you are drinking all the time, your liver (and all your other organs) need some extra love. I encourage you to try the recipes I have included and find some interesting cookbooks to explore. Reading about nutrition and health can be a fun new hobby when you decide to let go of alcohol and all its toxicity.

I personally have always loved smoothies and used to buy them pre-made at the store. When I stopped drinking, I started regularly having a morning smoothie that I made at home. This meant I was starting my day with something healthy that included lots of greens and super foods. I was making the conscious decision to heal myself from the inside out. Smoothies were a great way to get in some good nutrition. I have included my favorite smoothie recipe below:

This recipe makes 2 to 3 servings. Use frozen bananas and blueberries as this will make your smoothie nice and cold.

GORGEOUS GREEN SMOOTHIE

2 or 3 cups coconut/almond milk
3-4 cups of greens (I usually do a combo of spinach and lettuce or kale)
1 Tb chia seeds
1 Tb hemp seeds
1 Tb protein powder (your choice)
1Tb green powder (your choice)
1 1/2 - 2 frozen chopped bananas
1 1/2-2 tsp nut butter
1 1/2 tsp blueberries

Place all ingredients in your high-speed blender and blend for 40 seconds.

~

When you make the decision to quit drinking and you stick with it, your body will probably have some major sugar cravings. Your system is used to its regular alcohol sugar fix, even if you just drink alcohol on the weekends.

I remember asking one of my newly sober friends if she had lost a ton of weight when she got off booze and she said she had actually gained some weight initially because she started a nightly ice cream habit. I also had some sugar cravings when I quit drinking and I decided to make my own healthy ice cream. It became a favorite around our house and we still have it a few times a week. Luckily, we had some banana trees in our backyard which made this even more fun to make! You won't believe how amazing this is.

CACAO BANANA ICE CREAM
This recipe makes two small servings or one large serving
2 frozen chopped bananas
1/2 cup of coconut/almond milk (use more or less depending on whether you want more ice cream consistency or milk shake)
1 tsp cacao powder
1 tsp cacao nibs

Place all ingredients in your high-speed blender and blend for 40 seconds.

OTHER DRINKS

I personally never got into the whole "mock-tail" trend. If you have tried them and find it fun, that is great. For me, it seems this is just another way to pretend to drink. If I really embrace the fact that I don't want or need alcohol, why would I want a mock-tail?

Mock-tails seem like pseudo hip drinks to give people something to do when they aren't doing what the "herd" does. I don't need a "faux" drink. I personally feel like this is used to appease the drinkers in my life and make them more comfortable with their own drinking. I prefer to ask for something I actually want to drink rather than acting like I am a boozer when I'm not. I am proud of the fact I don't drink as I am putting my health first.

In my opinion, these actions just perpetuate the whole "I'm missing out vibe." This puts you in this place of trying to fit in with something you no longer want. Mentally this is confusing. When you are retraining your brain around alcohol, you don't want to continue to buy into the whole drink culture. By engaging in these activities, you are still telling yourself you really want to drink but can't. You are also telling others the same thing. Instead of letting them know how great you feel and how you couldn't care less to have a toxic beverage. When you order a mock-tail you give the message you still want to drink. This serves no one.

When I stopped drinking, I really started loving tea. I had always dabbled in tea, but in the evenings, tea became my new go to beverage. There are so many caffeine-free options on the market now. Teas you can drink at night that won't interfere with the good sleep you are going to get once you stop drinking and aren't waking up at 2am with the dreaded hangover shame. You will most likely also start drinking more water as you become more active and healthy. You can put lemons, oranges, grapefruits, watermelon or other fruits in your water bottle to jazz things up. I also started drinking mushroom coffee blends. These have some caffeine, so I recommend these as morning drinks. They have blends of mushrooms and adaptogen herbs. They are delicious. Green tea is very good for you and there are so many varieties! Matcha is a new favorite of mine. I will often have a cup after coffee in the morning.

Seltzer water is always a nice treat. I personally stopped drinking seltzer on a regular basis as I found they left me a bit bloated. They are a fun on occasion though. The sky is the limit in regard to drinks. I recommend finding what you like and if you are going to a party where people will be drinking alcohol, ask for tea, coffee, seltzer, or bring your own and be proud. Don't feel like you have to pretend to drink just to please others. Part of embracing a sober mind state is staying clear and remembering you are on a new path, why pretend to do what you used to do?

Be honest with yourself and others. Authenticity is key to a life of peace and grace. Who knows, someone on the fence regarding their own drinking might join you in ordering a cup of tea at a party. You may give them the permission they need to not imbibe. As long as we keep pretending to be in agreement with the toxicity of alcohol and all things related to alcohol, we are a part of the drinking culture. Be part of the new culture. People who aren't duped anymore by the lies society tells us about drinking. People who have woken up to the devastation and misery alcohol causes. People who are consciously choosing to not participate any more.

18

HICCUPS ALONG THE WAY

Time can be your friend or foe when you make the decision to quit drinking. Maybe you have tried to quit and a bit of time passes and this little voice inside your head says, "Hey, it's ok, you've been doing so well with this, you don't have any issues with alcohol. You can just drink sometimes. Everyone else drinks." The truth is everyone else is in the same boat as you. NO ONE is immune to the destruction of alcohol, so the urge to follow the herd is wrong. Many people are experiencing a similar mental battle concerning their own drinking, they just aren't talking about it for fear of being labeled an alcoholic. You don't have anyone to talk to about your concerns or your recent efforts and you realize everyone else you know is still doing it, so why not? You also have forgotten all the reasons you stopped drinking as time passes on. Your reasons for stopping are further away from you than the bottle of wine down the street. So you take a drink and start the whole process over again and then in a week, a month, or even a year down the road, you find yourself in the same place again. Wanting to stop drinking because of all the negative repercussions.

Use the knowledge you have about how drinking affects you in a negative way. It is similar to seeing the future. It is inevitable. If you currently want to stop drinking because you realize it is harmful and keeping you from your best life, you won't ever be able to view drinking as "fun" again. You will always want to stop. This is the perfect time to train your mind to tell yourself a different story. If for some reason those drinking urges come up, you can tell yourself something like this - "My life is a million times better when I don't drink. There is no way I want to ingest that stuff. If I take a drink, it might be fun for about 5 minutes but then there is nothing but misery." Then you say your mantra : "No thanks, I don't drink."

Why continue the misery? Get off the merry go round of this "on again, off again" relationship with alcohol. Breaking up for good is what gives you your life back. As long as you still have it as an option in the back of your mind, you will never truly be free of it. Your mind needs to get on board with the fact that drinking is just something you no longer do.

This is how time can become your friend. You are learning from the past and not forgetting. It is so very easy to fall into old patterns. This is one way that a meditation practice is so helpful. Once you become more mindful, you can stop these thoughts in their tracks and create a new story for yourself. Once you learn how to focus your mind, you can use that newfound focus to make positive changes.

~

Denial is another common hindrance in regard to leading a sober life. When I started sharing my book idea with close friends, many of them said they really wanted to quit drinking but couldn't imagine saying, "Never again." They were excited about a book that could help change their mindset and patterns. Most of them said they really didn't find alcohol fun anymore, but they also didn't know how to fully quit. They each said they didn't feel they had much of a "problem." All of them knew I drank less than they did and watching me quit (when it didn't look like I had a major problem), helped them examine their own drinking. They repeatedly said they really didn't want alcohol in their lives but yet it was still there. This is called denial. If you desire to quit drinking, but you haven't fully quit, you are in denial. One of the definitions of denial is: The refusal of something requested or desired. This is where your mind comes into play. You desire to quit but your subconscious mind isn't on board because your drinking is now a habit (or for some even a hobby).

Most of us think like this- We know plenty of people who drink more than we do which leads us to believe we don't have a "problem"and so we continue to drink. We do this even though alcohol is adding nothing positive to our lives. We don't think we are alcoholics or to the point where we need AA, so why stop now? The smartest decision you can make is to quit before you need AA. Before your life spins out of control, before you are chemically addicted to alcohol, before alcohol robs you of all of your personal power and possibly the people you love. If you are reading this and you aren't chemically addicted to alcohol yet but have a psychological addiction to alcohol, my question to you is this- what are you waiting for? Are you waiting until you do have a chemical addiction? Are you waiting until your relationships completely fall apart? Are you waiting until you start missing work due to hangovers and lose your job? Are you waiting for someone else to tell you that you need help? Take your power back and make the decision yourself.

Visualize yourself ten years down the road and picture how your life will look if you quit drinking today. Then take a moment and imagine yourself ten years down the road if you continue to drink. How will your life look? How are your relationships? How do you feel about yourself? Be honest with your answers.

~

For some people, counting sober days can be helpful, for others it can be a hiccup along the path to sobriety. We all have sober friends who let us know how long they have been sober. 30 days, 60 days, 10 years etc… Initially this is important, and it can feel good to count days and feel super proud of yourself. Stopping drinking in a world where most people drink is something to be proud of. You should feel great about yourself and the fact that you made one of the best decisions of your life when you gave up alcohol! I realize in some organizations they use this "counting sober days" method to give newly sober people hope that sobriety is possible for everyone. In my opinion, although this can be helpful, this method also trains your mind to continue to obsess and think about alcohol. I prefer to have the view that my natural state is a sober one. I don't need to count days that I have been without alcohol as alcohol is no longer important to me. I don't read about alcohol, blog about alcohol or talk about it unless someone asks. I thought about alcohol a lot while writing this book and it was a hugely therapeutic process, but after that I moved on. I no longer want to give alcohol any energy, interest, or power. By all means if counting days works for you, keep it up! However, if you don't find it works. Let it go. Some people get really tripped up if they start drinking again and the thought of starting all over counting days keeps them from getting sober. For some, a new paradigm is needed. An approach that lets go of counting days. One that doesn't focus on alcohol but chooses to focus on other things.

When I decided to quit drinking, I of course counted the days at first because it was so new to me and this is what society told me to do. Friends would ask, have you still not had any wine? How long has it been? I figured it needed to be like my birthday now, a date I forever remembered. Eventually, I quit keeping track. I prefer to focus on the rest of my life and the amazing future ahead. Yes, we learn from our history and it's important, but why stay stuck there? After about a month or two of being sober, alcohol was no longer taking up my headspace and I rarely thought about it unless someone asked me. I did the same thing when I quit smoking cigarettes. When I quit smoking 25+ years ago, at first I counted days and honestly for about a year, I still wanted one and now I have no clue of the exact date I quit. I know around what year, but just like alcohol, cigarettes are no longer part of my life. I don't give them thought or energy. Keeping track of something I no longer want to think about makes no sense to me. Again, it sets up this mind state of "I've gone 60 days without this substance I really want." If I train my mind to believe I no longer want alcohol, why keep track? So I can tell others? So I can brag with the facade of being helpful? This would definitely inflate my own ego, but does it truly serve others? Do they really need to know exactly how many days I have been sober, or vegan, or cigarette free?

How is this helpful? All people need to know is that there are groups of us that choose not to drink, and we are happier and healthier because of it. I want to inspire people to live a healthier life without making them feel like they are starting low on the totem pole. I want to let people know once they choose to give up alcohol, they are all set. Once they let it go, they enter a new reality where alcohol no longer takes their mental energy (including counting days).

19

OTHER ADDICTIONS

My husband, son, and I were in a documentary called Childhood 2.0. This film is about kids and the digital age. It's very eye opening regarding the tech world and how difficult it can be to navigate. One thing I realized while watching the film is that we will never be able to help our children with internet/social media addiction until we give up our own addictions. As always, our children are watching us. They will do what we do, not what we say.

I deactivated my Facebook account several years ago when my son made a comment about my addiction to it. He was right! How could I expect him to act differently? I was setting a horrible example. Just like with alcohol, I couldn't expect him not to drink if I was a drinker. Addiction comes in many forms. We must live our lives with vigilant mindfulness and become aware of where our time, energy, thoughts, and focus are directed. When we are mindless, we become slaves. Slaves to drugs, alcohol, and even technology. True strength and balance emerge from a mindful life. Being aware of our choices in every moment and teaching our children to do the same. I remember when I deactivated my Facebook account, I felt really lonely for several months. I went through a kind of depression and disconnect. My brain had gotten used to the extra dopamine pumping through. This was a real withdrawal, just like a drug. I also had to "leave the herd" as just about everyone I know is on Facebook. Just like when I quit drinking, I was doing something different, something outside the "norm". Normal isn't always better. I definitely would never have written this book if I hadn't cut out that addiction. I wouldn't have had time. Social media was sucking my time and energy more than I even realized.

Once you begin to let go of unhealthy habits and addictions, you will start noticing time suckers and energy vampires (not just human ones but technology and other substances as well). Our time and energy are precious and using them in productive ways leads to a more positive, healthy, and balanced life. Once again, this is where meditation comes into play. As you begin to meditate you will become more familiar with your own energy and thoughts. You will take this awareness into everyday life and become more selective with your preferences. Choices about who to hang around with, what to eat and drink, when to be online and when to do other things, etc…You will be much more in tune with yourself and what your nervous system needs. Your decisions will start to reflect this new intuition. This is one way meditation makes giving up things like alcohol or any other addiction a bit easier. You will start to have more self-love. You will no longer want to hurt your mind, body, and spirit. You will be the one in charge of your life, instead of being guided by what commercials and ads tell you to do. You will be less plugged into technology and more plugged into spirit. Spirit is the navigator you want, not a capitalistic society who just wants you to spend money on the latest thing they tell you that you need in order to be happy. Plugging into spirit instead of technology is one way you gain freedom.

20

EMBRACE SOBRIETY

I am not embarrassed that I no longer drink. In fact, I am proud to be a non-drinker. I have noticed many people who don't drink often make excuses as to why they don't do what everyone else seems to be doing. They say they have allergies or are on a special diet, or they make excuses, proclaiming that alcohol doesn't agree with them, etc... Sometimes these statements are true, but oftentimes people just feel uncomfortable telling others they prefer to be sober.

Why is alcohol the only drug we feel we need to make excuses regarding why we don't do it? How crazy is that? Having to constantly explain why you don't want to ingest a toxic poison that makes you feel like crap. Regularly feeling pressured by everyone around you, and feeling like you need to explain why you prefer not to drink.

Times are changing. Years ago, if you said you didn't drink, people instantly assumed you were an alcoholic. This may still be the case in certain circles, but there's a growing number of people who understand the negative repercussions of alcohol and are shifting to the sober life. I have found if I just say, "No thanks, I don't drink," it can sometimes lead to interesting conversations. I once had a friend ask why I no longer wanted to drink wine and I just told her the truth. I said, "I just don't find it fun anymore." She paused a minute and then said, "I don't find it fun anymore either." I could tell from her pause that my comment had made her think. The honest approach is the best way to communicate with people. You never know who you may be helping. Maybe they have been considering stopping but don't know how or don't have any support. Making up excuses and lying about why you don't drink only feels weird and doesn't serve you or anyone else. Embrace your newfound strength and truth and let it inspire others.

Gone are the days of feeling like a weirdo for not getting wasted. Instead, there will be people who envy your ability to say no to alcohol and want to know how you do it. I remember always being curious about people who could go to a dinner party and/or celebration and not drink when everyone else was. I wondered how they could be having any fun and if they secretly wished they could drink. Now I am in on their secret. They are actually the ones having fun because they are present and in their power. Not giving their power away to a drug only to be left hungover and miserable the next day. They have figured out that life is short.

How many more days do you want to waste being hungover? How many more moments will you miss because you are too buzzed to be fully present with what is actually happening. Time doesn't stand still and before you know it, a decade will go by that you might barely remember. Better to realize that sober really is the new sexy.

21

DRAMA + TRIGGERS

Drama follows drinkers and drug addicts like moths to a flame. I never realized the drama I was attracting into my life until I quit all drugs and alcohol. I had a few toxic relationships that were huge zappers of my energy. Just like the alcohol, I was allowing certain people to take from me and not give much in return. I noticed once I gave up drinking that I didn't have any patience for friends who tried to start drama.

You know the type. The drama queens, negative nellies, just plain old energy robbers. They were depleting my life force and I continued to allow it. I had certain friends who would call or text and try to start fights with me. They were drinking and wanted to let their anger out on someone. Once I got sober, I quit playing this game as I realized it was another energy drain. One more way that alcohol caused conflict. I no longer wanted any part of unnecessary drama or anger due to alcohol and its toxic nature. My friendships changed drastically once I stopped drinking as these particular friends were accustomed to me playing the game and returning the negative energy. Once I was less reactive to their dramas, they lost interest in me as they no longer had an angry friend to banter with. How boring to have a real conversation with someone who was growing and changing. They wanted me to stay the same. To not grow and thrive but to be the same person they had always known with the same reactions. I'm sure it was scary to them for me to shift my paradigm. Watching me become more healthy was a reminder to them of their own dysfunction and toxicity. Instead of being curious or supportive, most of these particular friends dropped out of my life. Part of my impetus in writing this book was thinking of these dear friends of mine who are still suffering and in the throes of addiction. I want for them what I now have. A life that isn't filled with the anguish that alcohol causes. The extra negativity, drama, and stress that doesn't need to be in your life.

If you aren't setting boundaries and learning to say no to these people, your health will suffer. Even texting can be toxic. Do you have a particular friend who will text you multiple times over and over until you respond? They act like you are a paid employee and need to be at their every beck and call. This is an energy drain! Friends should respect your time and understand you will respond when you have a free moment. This isn't to say you should play games and ignore the people you care about. Don't be a flake. Respect and value your time and the time of others.

When you stop drinking, you get your power back, and this starts to infiltrate into all aspects of your life. You realize all the other things and people that have been leaching your energy. You will become more empowered to say no and learn how significant healthy boundaries are for a peaceful life. Healthy friends will understand this, and the unhealthy drama queens will start to leave your life. Remember, you aren't just giving up toxic substances, but also toxic people. As these people exit your life, you will have more time and energy for important matters and creative endeavors.

In addition to sorting out the drama in your life once you get sober, you will also need to figure out your "triggers". Triggers are those things, places, and people who might encourage you to drink again. One of the biggest triggers for many of us can be some of our very best friends. All of my nearest and dearest high school and college friends are big drinkers. I met all of them when I was a drinker, so of course this is what we did together. Many (but not all) of my yoga friends are also drinkers. Although with this group of friends, I usually did other things like hiking, coffee, or yoga. They weren't really triggers for me as we really never drank together. The friends I have known since I was a child presented a completely different situation. Drinking wine was our thing! I had major concerns about this when I stopped drinking. I still loved and adored these friends and I wondered if our relationships would change or disappear altogether. I definitely wasn't interested in plopping down on the couch and watching these friends get loaded on wine. This wouldn't be fun for anyone. Instead, we started doing different things together. Catching a yoga class, going to the movies, going swimming, meeting for lunch or coffee. This really wasn't a big deal because most of these friends were curious about how I had quit drinking. This led to really great conversations that actually strengthened our relationship. We no longer had the same old, "Let's get drunk" scenario. I wasn't trying to change or preach to them about alcohol. I was just being myself. Mostly they honored my metamorphosis, and some were even inspired by it. Being authentic is key to any real friendship. I found when I was true to myself and my utmost health, the friends who loved me were nothing but supportive. You may find yourself with some negative friends who are jealous and not happy with your new take on life. Let them go with love and open the door to new friends who have your best interests in mind. As you begin to heal, the circle of friends you have may change. This is another indication that your mindset has shifted in a more positive direction. Like attracts like. You will begin to attract healthy friends who enjoy doing some of the new hobbies you have.

A whole sober world opens up to you once you let go of the old. This doesn't always mean you have to let go of dear friends you have had for ages. Sometimes this will happen, and that is ok. People often resist change as it makes them uncomfortable. Just remember, life is about growing and adapting. Never stay the same just to make others comfortable. This is part of reclaiming your power.

I actually had an interesting situation pop up after I broke up with alcohol. One of the friends who inspired me to quit drinking had started imbibing again right when I stopped. I wasn't aware of this and I messaged her to let her know I had quit. I wanted to tell her how amazing I felt. There was silence on the other end. Then she quit calling me for a couple of weeks. I knew she had started drinking again. She was embarrassed to tell me which made me really sad for her. I was positive at some point she would have to start the whole process of quitting all over again. I wasn't surprised she was back to it because when she told me she quit drinking she said, "I'm not saying I won't drink ever again." I realized when she said those words that she was just taking a break and not really ready to fully commit to quitting. When someone allows it to still be an option, they will most likely drink again. This experience was profound to me as it taught me we really are only responsible for ourselves. This friend had been an inspiration for me, hopefully now I could be one for her. That is what friends do. We might not be on the same page at the same time, but we can support one another. I certainly wasn't going to start drinking again just because she now was. I knew at some point she would want to get sober, as she had already realized how damaging alcohol was to her life. Once you have this realization about alcohol, you can't go back to the "ignorance is bliss phase."I was concerned that her next "aha" moment might not be as forgiving as her first one. She didn't have a "rock bottom" moment the first time she gave up alcohol. Just a mildly embarrassing situation that forced her take a look at her drinking habits. Hopefully nothing catastrophic would happen to her this time around. That is the problem with drinking too much, you never know what disaster is around the corner.

Once sober, you will gain clarity about who your true friends are. Once the drunk goggles are removed it, you will be more selective about who you spend your time with and what activities you participate in.

If you do have particular friends who are still very toxic, it can affect your own energy. You need to "cut the cord" to protect yourself. This section of the book might feel a bit "woo woo" to you if you haven't been in yoga or esoteric circles. However, I must include it as I feel it has played a key role in shifting my mindset in regard to alcohol. Try to keep an open mind and realize the world is much bigger than what you imagine it to be.

We are more than just this body. There is a world of energy all around us that affects us spiritually, emotionally, and psychically. I personally have always been very empathic and feel energy. Even though I have studied many books on the subject, I haven't always been mindful about protecting my own energy and boundaries. When I was shifting my mind about alcohol, I realized I also needed to check in with my energy body and make some changes. In the past, I would read books on the subject, try out some practices and then forget about them. I realized once I committed to a daily mediation practice, I was in fact cleaning up my energy without knowing it. When you meditate you start to become very familiar with your own energy field. Meditating gives an instant lift to your system and you move from a possible negative vibration into the positive. This leaves you feeling better and then you start noticing what things in your life take you out of this alignment. You begin to naturally make more healthy choices for yourself and certain toxic friendships and substances begin to leave your life. These friendships and substances are not attracted to the new positive vibration you have going on. Like attracts like and as you clean up your own energy body, you clean up your life.

Since everything is energy, it can be a powerful practice to implement some psychic cord cutting. We are all connected through energy. Most of us don't think about this very often , but we are attached psychically to people and substances. This is great if we want these things or people in our life but what happens if we no longer want a particular person or substance around anymore and they just won't leave? This is where psychic cord cutting comes into play. These cords can be very thick and run very deep, especially with family, close friends, or substances you have had around for a long time.

Around the time when I was making the choice not to drink, I realized I needed to clean up my own energy. I had some relationships that were were draining me on a deep level. When you are being energetically drained by someone on a consistent basis it is called "energy vampirism." You are allowing certain people to suck your life force on a daily basis. This can leave you feeling depressed, anxious, and confused. This situation is not uncommon. There are energy vampires all around us. Most of the time people are not even aware they are doing this. They are just completely drained of their own energy and must suck it out of others. This especially true if you hang around people with drug habits. They needed to suck other's energy as they barely any of her own life force left.

 Here is one way to protect your energy and clear out any "hitchhikers"-

Find a comfortable seated position and take a few deep breaths. Visualize a bright white light above your head. Imagine any negative energy leaving you and let the white light surround and fill you, bringing in positive energy.

Say the following statement out loud or create your own

statement-" I own my energy. Any entity or energy that is draining me does not have my permission to remain in my mind, body, or spirit. Leave now and do not return. Through the protection of (choose your own spiritual term) You can say God, Highest Vibration, Jesus, Light, (whatever you resonate with) then say- "I command this to be."

When I used this practice right after I quit drinking, I felt instant relief. No joke. It was like a weight lifted off me. I felt like myself again. The crazy thing is, my desire for alcohol dropped tremendously. I know it sounds insane but it is completely true. Whatever toxic cords I had with anyone were dropped and I felt better. This was instant feedback that this works. I now make it a regular practice to do weekly psychic cord protection practices in addition to my meditation. I respect and protect my own energy and the energy of others. Just like brushing my teeth or drinking my greens, it is a part of my routine. Energy work is key to a healthy, vibrant life.

The substances in our lives take up psychic energy as well. Therefore, if you plan on "drinking mindfully" (as they say in some circles), you will continue to have psychic ties to alcohol. It is most definitely robbing you of precious energy. When you are still drinking "on occasion" you are directing a lot of energy into those moments. Best to completely cut the cord and be done with it. Alcohol doesn't deserve your thoughts or energy. If you have decided it is harmful and has already caused negativity in your life. Why still treat it like some kind of reward that you only get on certain occasions? This is sending a mixed message to your subconscious mind. A message to yourself that you still like drinking, that you feel it has something positive to offer you, like it is a special a treat. I personally see it for what it is. Not a reward or a treat but a substance that does nothing to enhance my life but only hurts it. As long as you continue to put alcohol on some kind of pedestal it still has power. Just like I wouldn't "sometimes" date an abusive guy, just because I felt like seeing him. He might decide to punch me on that date. Why would I mess around with alcohol when it has shown me its evil ways? Why would I want that in my life anymore, even if only sometimes? I don't do cocaine or heroin sometimes. I don't smoke cigarettes sometimes. How and why is alcohol any different? Once you decide something is unhealthy for you, why have it "mindfully" sometimes? This makes zero sense.

Cut the cord and be done with it. Only then will you have true freedom. I believe the reason most people choose the route of "sometimes" instead of full abstinence, is because of the pressure they feel in certain social situations. We want to feel part of the "herd." We want acceptance and love. Instead, find self love and carve your own path.

In addition to sorting out out toxic friends and substances. You will also realize places can trigger you to drink. I always wanted to live by the ocean. We finally moved to the beach a few months before I decided to quit drinking. I never thought in a million years the beach would be the place where I would get sober. Our street was even named after a drink. In fact all the streets in our neighborhood were named after drinks. There's Margarita St., Medina St, Corona St, etc… How ironic I decided to give up alcohol while living there. I have always associated the beach with drinking. As a child we would vacation at the beach every summer. For the grownups, this meant a constant flow of alcohol. Then when I became an adult, every spring break, summer trip, or any kind of beach vacation involved considerable amounts of alcohol. I was actually nervous about living at the beach as I had already decided to cut back. I knew living in a place that felt like a permanent vacation was a recipe for disaster when it came to my drinking. The first month or so it was a challenge. I wanted to drink daily and had to really hold back the urge. I regularly persuaded my husband to have beers on the beach with me, even though he really wasn't interested. He eventually started to crave a nice cold one most days. The beach and alcohol kind of go together if you get into that routine. I guess you could say the beach used to be a "trigger" for me. This happened because I had a pattern of always drinking while at the beach. I needed to once again retrain my mind.

Before I even made the decision to stop drinking, I trained my subconscious mind to start viewing the beach and our new home as a very calm and healing place. I began connecting with the jungle nature vibe. I would bike, walk the beach, look for shells, walk the dog in the neighborhood, exercise on the beach, etc. I was connecting with this new area in a more "spiritual" way. Instead of just focusing on the beach as a place to kick back and have some beers, I started associating the ocean with feeling healthy. Again, this shift happened in my mind before it happened in my reality. The more I mentally noted how healthy, calm, and centered I felt in this new environment, the more I started to associate the beach and our new home with health and healing instead of visualizing our new home as "party central."

You see it really is all about shifting your paradigm. Obviously, this technique may not work for all of your trigger places. I don't frequent bars as the focus in a bar is on drinking, it is pretty challenging to find other things to do while there. Why would I even go? Once you stop drinking your vibration shifts anyway and you won't energetically be drawn to places where the focus is solely on drinking. I am referring to places that have turned into triggers because of personal patterns. I turned the beach into a trigger because I had always partied while at the beach. It was quite easy to see all the wonderful other things to do on the beach once I shifted my thoughts about it.

What are some triggers for you? Vacation spots? Friend's

houses? Holidays? Maybe even your own home at "happy hour." I think this last one is a major one for most people. If you have always come home from work at 5pm and had a cocktail and/or glass of wine, of course this is a huge trigger for you!

The solution is simple. Instead of going straight home after work which puts you in your normal routine. Join a gym, start going to a yoga and/or meditation class, go hiking or walking, or biking. If exercise isn't your thing, go to a library or a bookstore, or even grocery shopping. You can replace the habit of always drinking after work with anything else. I personally didn't struggle with this one as I wasn't a daily drinker (most of the time). I think if I had been, I would definitely have needed to go somewhere other than home at the "witching hour." When you choose another hobby, your body time clock will lose the urge to drink at 5pm (or whenever you typically used to drink). After a few days, this new routine will become established and you will lose the desire to drink at "happy hour." You will now have meditation hour, yoga hour, running hour, or grocery hour, etc... Your drinking habit will be replaced with something else. No longer will your own home be a trigger, but a place of comfort and nourishment. A true retreat from the world. I personally love to have tea and meditation sessions in the evenings now, even on the weekends. This is my new ritual and I have become quite the tea connoisseur. The very best part of this is a sharper mind, a happier spirit, and no hangovers or bad feelings about myself the next day.

22

HAVING A VISION

A few months before I finally quit drinking, I was feeling middle aged and not happy about it. Instead of looking forward to the years ahead, I felt depressed and lost. I was grateful to be alive but felt directionless. I decided to recommit myself to a life of total health and fitness, not just physically but also mentally. I had been redirecting my thoughts from negative to positive. Through these practices I became more adept at noticing negative patterns of behavior. I am convinced all of this mind preparation helped me have a more streamlined process to sobriety than others I had read about. My reality had caught up with my mind. The better I started feeling mentally, the less I wanted or needed drugs.

About a year prior to stopping alcohol, I participated in a 4 week course that involved meditation, dialogue and intent visioning. During the course we made a vision board. I had always thought of vision boards as a waste of time (even though I had never done one.) I'm not sure why I had such preconceived ideas about these boards. I just thought they seemed very "cheesy." I had been dreading the activity and thought I wouldn't enjoy it. As it turns out I had a blast! The activity was really cool. As a group, we dove into our meditation and then after about 30 minutes, we each had a poster board and several magazines in front of us. We were instructed to choose images we were drawn to and glue them to our poster board. The teacher told us not to judge why we were drawn to something but to just go with our intuition. I created my board and it was actually really fun. It felt good to focus on myself and my desires. The other participants and I shared our boards and discussed why we thought we were drawn to certain photos. Then I took the vision board home and hung it in my clothes closet where I was sure to see it every day. Eventually I forgot about it, barely noticing it as I passed it each day. Apparently, the visions were still in my mind, because a year later I looked at the board and noticed literally EVERY SINGLE IMAGE on the board was currently in my life! I had placed photos of the beach, palm trees, waves, surfboards, even a photo of a French phrase. That same year we moved to a beach house after a stint in Europe where we spent a lot of time in France! I will never make fun of vision boards again. Also, there was definitely no alcohol on my vision board. Our thoughts are so very powerful! Now each year, making a vision board is a fun activity I look forward to. I view it as an essential element of making the "blueprint" of my life. I encourage you to create your own vision board as part of your path to sobriety.

What are your current dreams and desires? What images portray how you want to think and feel? The images don't have to be material objects. You can place images that portray happiness, love, freedom, joy, positivity, etc… create a board that describes the way you want to feel and who you want to be.

When you become mindful that you have control of how you want your life to be, you gain so much power. You can use this strength to stop drinking. Don't envision yourself as a drinker anymore. Put beautiful images on your board and watch at they begin to flow into your life.

23

SOBER IS THE NEW SEXY

I'll let you in on a little secret. You are not sexy when you are drunk. Alcohol tricks your brain into thinking you are smarter, hotter, and even more funny when you drink. Don't listen to the alcohol. There is absolutely nothing sexy about a drunk person. Try staying sober for an evening around a bunch of drunk people and test my theory. Slurring, stumbling and sloppiness are not sexy. Sober is sexy in a way that drunk can never be. Sexy is focused, smart, confident, self-assured, genuinely funny, clear, and kind. Actually, these are all qualities you lose when you drink. So, my question is, who do you want to be in this life? The choice is yours each and every day. Do you want to continue to choose a road that is not productive or sexy?

Maybe you only have one or two glasses each night, so you don't get drunk and take on the above mentioned qualities. However, bit by bit, day by day, alcohol changes you. Bit by bit, day by day, you want and need more alcohol, and bit by bit, day by day, you start to lose your true essence which is far more sexy than the drunk version of yourself.

Think of the qualities you want to embody as a person. Do you want to be smarter, more confident, have more self-love, be more focused and kind? Does a drinking habit help you obtain those qualities? If not, then why do you drink? "Because it is fun," is the wrong answer. When you are being honest and mindfully examining your life, you will come to realize there is nothing fun in losing your true nature and your connection to source. There is nothing exciting about not coming from a centered place but a drunk one. So, the question is, how is alcohol serving you? Ponder that for a moment. Embrace the fact that you deserve a better life, you deserve happiness, you deserve prosperity, you deserve love, you deserve harmony, you deserve all the blessings you are finally aware of once you become sober and present.

24

LAST CALL

We all know the term "Last Call." The final drink you have at the end of a long evening of partying. Your eyes are blurry, your brain is jumbled, you might not even be aware of your surroundings. I compare this to how I felt when I finally had the "Last Call" of my life, my final drink. In that moment I felt lost, out of control, despondent, angry, and wondered who I was anymore. I had lost too much of myself to a horrible drug. So many moments, relationships, and dreams were ruined because I continued to make the choice to drink. Why was alcohol the last drug I said goodbye to? I quit cigarettes, pills, and pot all before I quit drinking. Alcohol was the one drug I continued to use over and over and over, telling myself it was only sometimes, telling myself it wasn't a problem, telling myself it was what everyone does, telling myself I could take it or leave it. I continued to lie to myself over and over about the repercussions of a life with alcohol. I now realize it was easy to delude myself because alcohol is socially accepted. All the other drugs I gave up have some kind of stigma attached to them, so they were easier to let go of. I'm rarely around cigarette smokers and most people I know keep their pot smoking a secret. Therefore, when I let go of these substances, they weren't constantly being offered to me. As we all know, this is not the case with alcohol. Alcohol is everywhere.

This is ONE reason alcohol is the most dangerous drug of all. We tell ourselves everyone does it, it's normal, it's under control, there is no problem. We continue to find others who drink more than we do, so we can feel better about our own drinking. We cling to our booze like we cling to no other substance or person in our life.

Then one day we look up and realize alcohol has all the power and control. All the energy that it takes to continue to lie to ourselves about our drinking is taking over our life, yet society still tells us it's ok, they tell us it's fun. Even when we know better, even when our own experience has told us otherwise. We plod along and continue to participate.

Until one day we don't.

FINAL THOUGHTS

I encourage you to look at your current situation and really think about whether alcohol truly adds happiness to your life. You can make a change. It doesn't have to be a dramatic moment. It can be as simple as just deciding "I don't drink anymore." This moment comes at different times for all of us and I'm not insinuating this will be an easy decision. However, once you make the decision, life actually becomes fun again. Unless you have a clinical addiction to alcohol and need medical assistance to help you quit, you are a decision away from having your life back. All the energy and attention you were giving to alcohol (even if just on the weekends) can now go into other hobbies and practices. You can choose hobbies that lead to true contentment, unlike excessive drinking which eventually will destroy you and those you love.

Something shifts inside you once you remove drinking alcohol from your life. Once you don't allow it to be an option, a whole new world opens up. I know this sounds bizarre and far-fetched but it is what happened to me and I don't think I am any different than you. I felt like I was living in some zombified world and now I am in the world of the living.

Maybe you also feel like you are drowning or spinning out of control. Take back ownership of your life. You can decide your next chapter. Letting go of your attachment to the hobby of drinking will give you your life and power back. No one can do this for you. The world wants you to keep drinking but don't fall for it. Look around and if you aren't happy, if you don't feel joy anymore, alcohol and your addiction to it might be the culprit. Don't just go on another "break" from it. Break up for good and don't look back! You know the saying, "Everything you want is on the other side of fear?" I have a new take on it, "Everything you want is on the other side of an addicted life." Free yourself from the chains of alcohol's grip before it cages you forever. You will feel a freedom you haven't felt since you were a child. This free feeling doesn't come from "breaks" from alcohol, it only comes from letting it go for good.

I like to view letting go of alcohol as if it were a balloon. I release it, watch it float for a while, and then it goes up up and away, never to be seen again. Eventually I don't even give it a thought. I know it's hard to imagine that feeling when you are in the grips of alcohol's allure. The best thing to do is to remember you are only a choice away from watching your own balloon float far far away. You just need to use your new Mantra- "No Thanks, I Don't Drink."

Sending you love, peace, and strength

Ashlee

ABOUT THE AUTHOR

Ashlee Dunn B.S. Elementary Education, has been a yoga teacher for 25 years. She has studied yoga, meditation, and philosophy extensively in India and the U.S. Ashlee has developed yoga programs, taught classes, and guided workshops and retreats for studios around the country. She has certifications in multiple forms of yoga. For the past several years, her primary focus has been meditation.

Ashlee FINALLY came to the realization that alcohol and other drugs were a hindrance to her spiritual practices. She broke up with alcohol and has never looked back. She now spends her time meditating, writing, hiking, hanging out with her family and helping others learn how to live a full-time yogic lifestyle instead of a part time one.

Ashlee currently resides in Melbourne Beach, Florida with her husband, son and Australian Shepherd. They love to travel, so by the time this book releases, they will most likely be living somewhere else. Stay in touch with her at www.ashleedunn.com or on Instagram @ashleeleighdunn